Francis of Assisi
Encounters
Sultan Malek al-Kamil

KATHLEEN A. WARREN, O.S.F.

Daring to Cross the Threshold

Francis of Assisi Encounters Sultan Malek al-Kamil

WIPF & STOCK · Eugene, Oregon

Wipf and Stock Publishers
199 W 8th Ave, Suite 3
Eugene, OR 97401

Daring to Cross the Threshold
Francis of Assisi Encounters Sultan Malek Al-Kamil
By Warren, Kathy, OSF
Copyright©2003 Academy of Our Lady of Lourdes
ISBN 13: 978-1-62032-421-9
Publication date 8/15/2012
Previously published by Sisters of St. Francis, 2003

Cover icon by Br. Robert Lentz, OFM

To our congregational foundress, Mother Alfred Moes,
whose courage to cross the threshold
of interfaith partnership
with Dr. William Worrall Mayo
gave birth to an institution of healing
that has benefited multitudes
from many lands, races, cultures and religions;

To my Norwegian, maternal grandmother,
Margaret Golberg,
whose deep love for her Lutheran tradition
and openness to Catholicism
taught me how to respect
what one does not necessarily embrace as one's own;

and
To my nieces and nephews:
Vaughn, Kara, Laura, Natalie, Jack, Stephanie, Mary,
Cole, Chase, and . . . ,
and the children of the world –
whose futures demand our crossing new thresholds.

Contents

Acknowledgements

In the fall of 2000 I began the Master's Program in Franciscan Studies at the Franciscan Institute, St. Bonaventure University. At that time I selected Interreligious Dialogue as my area of special focus. Little did I suspect how significant that particular specialization would become. One year later the events of September 11, 2001, highlighted the urgency for greater understanding among religious traditions. Specifically, the lack of understanding and acceptance between Muslims and Christians was suddenly catapulted into headlines around the world.

As I worked on various papers, and eventually the major project from which this book has evolved, it seemed that all the resources of the media – television, newspapers, magazines and the internet – were committed to assisting me. Daily the news was filled with reports of the Crusades, Islam, interreligious conflicts and steps toward dialogue. Exploring paradigms for serious dialogue, understanding and peace became critical.

Now, in the aftermath of war in Iraq, the need for understanding and respect between religious traditions and various cultures becomes ever more important. It is my hope that this small book might further that mutual respect which fosters peace and justice – God's desire for us and a gift that all races and religions seek.

I am tremendously grateful to the faculty of the Franciscan Institute for their unflagging support in this project. From the day I entered the program Sr. Margaret Carney, OSF, dean and director of the Franciscan Institute, has been relentless in her encouragement of this Interreligious focus. My gratitude is also extended to Fr. Michael Blastic, OFM Conv., who offered invaluable insights into the vision of Francis and the spirituality of both Francis and Islam. Brother Tony LoGalbo, OFM, launched me into this project. His research assignment eventually led me to a course in Ecumenism and Interreligious Dialogue offered at the *Centro Pro Unione* in Rome. There my work was enhanced by the expertise of Fr. James Puglisi, S.A. and Sr. Lorelei Fuchs, S.A

This book would never have appeared without the encouragement, support, and assistance of Fr. Michael Cusato, OFM, who served as the mentor for my project. His devotion to detail and excellence led me far beyond what I would have dared to undertake alone. His passion for exploring and proclaiming Franciscan history and encouraging others to do the same is well known to his students.

Even more significantly, each faculty member, all along the way, consistently embodied the true humility, minority, and fraternal spirit of Francis and Clare.

More recently, I worked with and learned from Sr. Roberta McKelvie, OSF, Managing Editor of Franciscan Institute Publications. Her continual encouragement and technical skill have been invaluable. Jean-François Godet-Calogeras graciously volunteered to take on the task of preparing the text for publication by formatting the entire work.

Lastly, none of this would have happened without the support and encouragement of my own congregation, the Sisters of St. Francis of Rochester, MN. They have wholeheartedly affirmed my full-time study and research. I am especially indebted to Sr. Dolore Rockers, OSF, Community Minister, and to her team: Sisters Geneva Berns, OSF, Barbara Haag, OSF, Monique Schwirtz, OSF, Avis Schons, OSF, and Jean Keniry, OSF. I am equally grateful to my Sisters Eleanor Granger, OSF, Valerie Usher, OSF, Ingrid Peterson, OSF, and Ramona Miller, OSF, for their gifts of friendship and absolute confidence in the value of this project.

Feast of Pentecost, 2003

Preface

During the waning months of 2002 and the dawning weeks of 2003, Pope John Paul II repeatedly urged the members of the international community to draw back from the brink of war and avoid unleashing a further cycle of violence upon our planet. The Holy Father firmly believed that there was another way, indeed multiple other ways short of military power, to resolve the intractable problems of human evil and injustice in the world. And that way was for human beings to choose to enter into dialogue with each other and thereby arrive at the peaceful resolution of those outstanding issues of conflict that threaten our fragile earth and its inhabitants. These increasingly urgent appeals of the Holy Father, moreover, were consistently grounded in the gospel of Jesus Christ and the broad contours of Christian history – both of which contend that war should be the last and the worst alternative to the resolving the problem of conflict among human beings.

John Paul II was not alone in this cry for peace. Leaders of most of the world's religious communities – as well as millions of people throughout the world – were likewise demanding that Washington and London cease its inexorable march toward war. Nor was the pontiff content to merely utter stern words; action was also imperative. He sent his personal representative, Cardinal Roger Etchegaray, to Baghdad to initiate a process of dialogue with the Iraqi leadership. He also sent Cardinal Pio Laghi to Washington on a similar mission. The Latin archbishop of

Baghdad, Jean Benjamin Sleiman, joined this swelling chorus of voices, calling for dialogue between the two parties. And the Holy Father welcomed the Deputy Prime Minister of Iraq, Tariq Aziz, in Rome for urgent discussions, prior to Aziz's visit to Assisi, the city of St. Francis, where he knelt at the tomb of the saint and, we are told, prayed for peace. Indeed, contrary to the actions of the leaders of the United States, Britain and Spain, each of these men – and countless others across the globe – had the courage to attempt to cross the threshold of misunderstanding and hate separating the Christian and Muslim populations of the world.

Sister Kathy Warren, O.S.F. came to the The Franciscan Institute on the campus of St. Bonaventure University in the fall of 2000 to begin a program that would lead to her receiving a Master's degree in Franciscan Studies in the spring of 2002. Early on in her studies, it became apparent to me that she, too, firmly believed that there was "another way" to resolve the problems created by human misunderstanding, evil intentions and sin: the way of creative dialogue and mutual respect. Already an advocate of inter-religious dialogue, Kathy began to see patterns for such conversations within the medieval Franciscan tradition. Her first attempt to delve into these waters resulted in a paper on the life and work of Ramón Lull, a late 13th century layman who, born into the rich, diverse yet sometimes contentious religious environment of Majorca – where the Christian, Muslim and Jewish communities lived in uneasy *convivencia* – had attempted throughout his long life to urge all three peoples to enter into dialogue with each other and thereby come to the truest Truth which God had planted within the collective human heart. Lull not only had close connections with the two great mendicant Orders of his day – the Friars Minor and Friars Preacher – but he also reportedly became a Third Order Franciscan later in life. Kathy rightly sensed that the grand vision of Ramón Lull was in some ways echoing a pre-existing tradition of dialogue and respect that took as its inspiration the legendary encounter of Francis of Assisi with the sultan Malek al-Kamil at Damietta in September 1219 at the height of the Fifth Crusade. This encounter served as a paradigm of how peoples who often regarded each other as "enemy" and "infidel" could cross the threshold of these hateful stereotypes and enter into fruitful dialogue and peaceful co-existence. Here was an event that truly demonstrated there was another way to resolve human problems and conflict.

Kathy's insight into the possibilities contained within the famous encounter in the sultan's tent resulted in this masterful paper which we all now have the privilege of reading, meditating upon and, hopefully, translating into actions "worthy of penance" in our own lives as we face the challenges to peace today. My hope is that her penetrating analysis of the encounter of Francis and the sultan – and its ramifications for our time – may help each one of us to cross the many thresholds of fear, misunderstanding and hate which we have learned and been taught so as to enter upon the holy ground of understanding, peace and right relationship which is nothing short of God's intentions for us all.

Michael F. Cusato, O.F.M.
The Franciscan Institute
1 May 2003

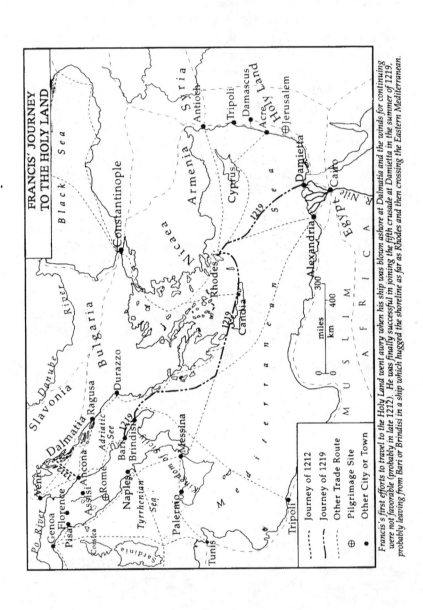

FRANCIS' JOURNEY TO THE HOLY LAND

Francis's first efforts to travel to the Holy Land went awry when his ship was blown ashore at Dalmatia and the winds for continuing were not favorable (probably in late 1212). He was finally successful in joining the fifth crusade at Damietta in the summer of 1219, probably leaving from Bari or Brindisi in a ship which hugged the shoreline as far as Rhodes and then crossing the Eastern Mediterranean.

Journey of 1212
Journey of 1219
Other Trade Route
⊕ Pilgrimage Site
• Other City or Town

Maps are taken from *Francis and Islam* by Jan Hoeberichts.
Used with permission of The Franciscan Press.

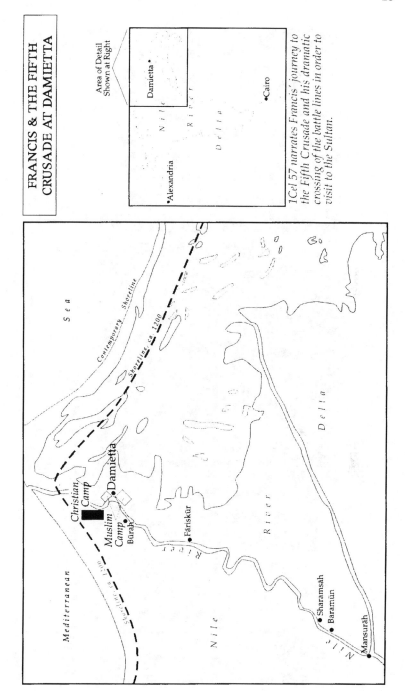

FRANCIS & THE FIFTH CRUSADE AT DAMIETTA

Area of Detail
Shown at Right

Damietta

Cairo

Nile

River

Delta

Alexandria

1Cel 57 narrates Francis' journey to the Fifth Crusade and his dramatic crossing of the battle lines in order to visit to the Sultan.

Mediterranean

Sea

Contemporary Shoreline

Shoreline ca. 1200

Shoreline ca. 1200

Christian Camp

Damietta

Muslim Camp

Būrah

Delta

Fāriskūr

River

Nile

NILE

Sharamsāh

Baramūn

Mansūrah

Inscription carved in marble: "There is no god but God and Muhammad is the Prophet of God." Egypt, 13th–15th centuries.

Introduction

The world finds itself at a critical juncture once again. Pope John Paul II has recently proclaimed: "It seems that war has been declared on peace!"[1] War and terror rage in cities and countrysides around the globe. Old ways are not bringing about the peace and justice so long-awaited by the world and so desperately needed. Where are the answers? What is the way? Four times in the past fifteen years –1986, 1993, 1999, 2002 – this same Pope has called world religious leaders together and invited them to witness to and pray for peace in that place recognized by many as the home of the peace-maker par-excellence, Francis of Assisi.

What was it about Francis that allowed him to live as such a powerful peacemaker? That question will be explored here by identifying the vision which directed Francis throughout his life and which attracted thousands of followers to him before he died. His was a vision of a "new way" of living. It asked nothing less than a complete upheaval of accepted societal and religious values and the embrace of a new reality: one of brotherhood and sisterhood expressed in a life of penance. The dichotomy between these two value systems is graphically illustrated by two statements. One, a belief held by Pope Innocent III, the reigning pontiff at the time of Francis' conversion; the other the belief that directed the life of Francis:

---

[1]Pope John Paul II, *Easter Message*, March 31, 2002.

Pope Innocent III	Francis of Assisi
"If anyone wants to follow me to the crown let him also follow me to the battle, which is now proposed as a test of faith for all people."	"Praised be You, my Lord, through those who give pardon for Your love, and bear infirmity and tribulation. Blessed are those who endure in peace for by You, Most High, shall they be crowned."
(*Quia maior*)	(*Canticle of the Creatures* 10)

In a time when thousands were heeding the call to join the Fifth Crusade, Francis was compelled by a different world-view, one rooted in the vision of Christ. The converted Francis dared to cross the threshold[2] into the camp of the Sultan of Egypt and there discovered new mysteries and new truths. Daring to cross over into the camp of those identified as "the enemy," Francis gained new insights about the human family. Daring to be exposed to new realities, Francis was willing to again embrace the stripping demanded by deeper conversion. His encounter with Sultan Malek al-Kamil was an unprecedented venture that continues to offer the world a bold paradigm for Interreligious Dialogue.

In order to understand the impact of Francis' crossing the Sultan's threshold, one must examine the results of that experience: alienation – with both members of his Order and with the official Church – as well as an expanded vision of universal fraternity that included not only non-christians, but the entire cosmos. Francis' experience of fraternal dialogue with the Sultan has much to say to us today about relating to those who profess a different faith, or a different world-view, or who simply live differently than we do. There are powerful messages from this peacemaker which transcend time and which have been waiting for centuries to be heard.

---

[2]Definitions of threshold include the concepts of crossing over to a new place as well as the entrance into or beginning point of something. Related to the term is the reality of threshing, the process of separating wheat from chaff, saving what is precious and discarding what is not.

The following exploration of the vision of Francis the peace-maker will examine some aspects of thirteenth-century Christendom and Islam, particularly in the context of the Fifth Crusade; the experience of Francis in Egypt, among both the crusaders and Saracens; and some of the beliefs of Islam that Francis would have encountered while in Egypt. The life of Francis after he left Egypt, with his vision deepened and expanded, contains significant implications for Interreligious Dialogue and peacemaking today; it also dares us to cross new thresholds.

Chapter 1

Setting the Stage:
The Fifth Crusade

Background for the call of the Fifth Crusade

On October 2, 1187, when Saladin seized Jerusalem, Christian control of the Holy Land came to an end. Unlike the vicious
and cruel slaughter of Jews and Muslims by the crusaders in
1099 (chronicled by both Christian and Muslim writers),
Saladin's treatment of the Christian population was relatively
humane and reasonable.[1] Although he returned the Church of

[1]Jane I. Smith summarizes the victory of the Crusaders: "The victory,
unfortunately, was accompanied by a vicious and cruel slaughter of
Jews and Muslims in the city. . . . Many Muslim writers . . . described
the carnage of the Christian massacre of Muslims, including many
religious leaders and Sufi mystics, as the acts of savage and cruel
western barbarians." *The Oxford History of Islam*, ed. John L. Esposito
(Oxford: Oxford University Press, 1999) 338. Relying on Penny Cole
and Jonathan Riley-Smith, Tomaz Mastnak also speaks of the
ruthlessness of the First Crusade. "The crusade was fashioned as a big
cleansing operation, and cleansing the holy places was posited as the
Christians' *point d'honneur*. According to Guibert of Nogent, Pope Urban
urged his armed brethren [. . .] to strive with 'utmost efforts to cleanse
the Holy City . . .' [in his report he also wrote that Urban told his
crusaders to] 'hasten to exterminate this vile race from our lands.'"
Tomaz Mastnak, *Crusading Peace: Christendom, The Muslim World,*

the Holy Sepulchre to Greek Orthodox custody, a number of churches were turned into mosques and Jerusalem was clearly, once again, a Muslim city. Henceforth Christianity and Islam would be engaged in a military conflict, both in the Holy Land and in Spain, for the next century.[2]

Newly elected Pope Gregory VIII, in October 1187, called for a Third Crusade to recapture the Holy City. This crusade yielded little except for securing Christian possession of a few coastal towns in Palestine and free access to Jerusalem for Christian pilgrims. In August 1198, Pope Innocent III (elected the previous January) called for the Fourth Crusade (1202-1204). This ended in a complete failure as it was detoured first to Yugoslavia then to Constantinople, ending with the capture, looting and division of the city by the crusaders. The tide began to turn for the Christians when they won a stunning victory over the Moors in southern Spain at Las Navas de Tolosa in July 1212.

In April 1213, Pope Innocent III wrote his encyclical, *Quia maior*, announcing his plans for a Fifth Crusade (1217-1221). Unlike previous crusades that were usually in the hands of civil authorities, Innocent decided that he, himself, would direct the Fifth Crusade, putting all the energies of the papacy and Christendom behind the effort. With the failure of the Fourth Crusade, due largely to insufficient funding, he prepared a comprehensive plan for a new offensive to secure the Holy Land. This detailed plan included everything from a tithing system to the granting of crusade indulgences to new preaching techniques. This same encyclical would also significantly affect the nascent Franciscan movement as well as Francis himself.

The encyclical was strong and clear. Innocent speaks of "the perfidious Saracens" who occupy the Holy Land of Jesus and who must be routed. Jan Hoeberichts, referring to *Quia maior*, says:

---

and Western Political Order (Berkeley: University of California, 2002) 127-128.

[2]Saladin leveled no retaliation on the Christians. Those who wished to leave the city were allowed to do so. Those who stayed could worship freely. Mass was celebrated as usual.

> He [Innocent] cried for help in the name and on behalf
> of Jesus Christ 'who when dying cried with a loud voice
> on the cross.' And as if this were not enough, Innocent
> continued that even at that very moment Christ cried
> out with his own voice, repeating the call of the Gospel:
> 'If anyone wants to come after me, let him deny himself
> and take up his cross and follow me,' – and so Innocent
> added – 'as if to say, to put it more plainly: If anyone
> wants to follow me to the *crown*, let him also follow me
> to the *battle*, which is now proposed as a test of faith for
> all people'[3] (italics mine).

Innocent's encyclical achieved the practical results of securing the necessary funding and personnel for his crusade. It also
was of great theological significance. In fact, as Jan Hoeberichts
has stated so well, "it constituted the climax of thinking about
the crusades."[4] *Quia maior* accomplished that by offering a
broad-based rationale for this call to arms. Highlights of his
impassioned call to crusade included:[5]

• the invitation of Christ to take up his cross and follow him
into battle thereby gaining eternal salvation symbolized most
forcefully by the use of the *tau* as the image of the crusader;

• reminding the people of their duty to observe the great com-
mandment of love and join in rescuing the thousands of Christians who were "weighed down by the yoke of most severe slavery";

• recalling that not only was Jerusalem held by the "perfidious Saracens" but that Mount Tabor had also recently been
taken. With these strongholds, Innocent feared that this ruth-
less enemy would, if not stopped now, gain control of the entire
area of the Holy Land, which Christians had held since the time
of the First Crusade;

• full forgiveness of sins (plenary indulgence) for those who
confessed: not only for those who actively participated in the
crusade, but also for anyone who paid for someone to go in their

[3]Jan Hoeberichts, *Francis and Islam* (Quincy: Franciscan Press, 1977)
9.

[4]Hoeberichts, *Francis and Islam* 9.

[5]This information is summarized from Hoeberichts, *Francis and Islam*
9-13.

place or who contributed monetarily to the crusade. Thus, the spiritual benefits of the crusade were available to all Christians (men and women).[6]

With such a call, the crusade movement was cast not merely as a military conquest but also as a religiously motivated operation. The crusade also supported the other major priority of Innocent's reign: church reform. Innocent proposed that God did not need the crusaders to liberate the Holy Land; that could be accomplished by God's will without their help. However, the crusade offered an opportunity for the Christians to attain their salvation. Reforming their lives by this type of dedicated service to God through the crusade was a means of attaining holiness.[7] In sum, this new army of Christ was fighting a

> holy and just war for the liberation of the Holy Land, Christ's inheritance which by right belonged to the Christians, and for the liberation of Jerusalem, the forerunner of the heavenly Jerusalem, in order to gain thereby their eternal salvation. This ideal was very attractive because it opened for knights and other lay people a way to salvation which placed them on the same level as the religious, while the activities which were asked of them fit well with what they were accustomed to doing in their normal, ordinary lives.[8]

The incredible clarity of this call to fight, subdue and wipe out the Saracens was in fact rooted in the justification presented

---

[6]James Powell notes that this inclusion of all Christians in the indulgence made it possible for everyone, not just the crusaders, to share in the moral preparation and penance of the crusade. "*Quia maior*'s extension of the spiritual benefits of the crusade broadened its links with the penitential system of the church and carried that system significantly closer to the goal enunciated at Lateran IV in the requirement for annual confession of sins." (*Anatomy of a Crusade 1213-1221*, [Philadelphia: University of Pennsylvania Press, 1986] 20).

[7]Powell, *Anatomy of a Crusade* 19.

[8]Hoeberichts, *Francis and Islam*, 15. James Powell adds that the development of the crusade in the 11th and 12th centuries was tied to an emerging lay spirituality, "which aspired to the monastic ideal of "*imitatio Christi*" and its pursuit in the gospel-inspired *vita apostolica*, with emphasis on evangelical poverty" (*Anatomy of a Crusade* 4).

a half century earlier by Bernard of Clairvaux. The boldness of Bernard's argument deserves to be reviewed since it clearly influenced Innocent's call to take up the sword against the Saracens. Hoeberichts relates the case presented by Bernard:

> To inflict death or to die for Christ is no sin, but rather an abundant claim to glory. In the first case one gains for Christ, and in the second one gains Christ himself. The Lord accepts with pleasure the death of the enemy as revenge, and gives himself with greater pleasure to the [fallen] knight as consolation. The knight of Christ, I say, may kill with confidence and die with greater confidence, for he serves himself when he dies, and serves Christ when he kills the enemy. The knight of Christ does not bear the sword without reason, for he is the minister of God for the punishment of evildoers and for the praise of the good. If he kills an evildoer, he is not the killer of a human being, but, if I may so put it, a killer of evil. He is simply the avenger of Christ towards evildoers and the defender of the Christians. Should he be killed himself, we know that he has not perished, but reached his goal. [. . .] When he inflicts death, it is to Christ's profit, and when he suffers death, it is for his own death Christ is glorified; in the death of a Christian the liberality of the king is revealed when the knight is called forward to be rewarded . . . I do not mean to say that the pagans are to be slaughtered when there is another way to prevent them from harassing and persecuting the faithful, but only that now it is better to kill them than that the rod of the sinners be lifted over the lot of the just.[9]

Thus Innocent highly concurs with Bernard's use of the scripture passage from Corinthians to justify and rally support for the first crusade: "Now is the favorable time, this is the day of salvation" (2 Cor. 6:1-2).

---

[9]Hoeberichts, *Francis and Islam* 16.

The Crusade Preacher

The chief means of presenting Innocent's call to crusade was through crusade preachers. Their importance cannot be over-emphasized. The preachers were well prepared to call the laity to an imitation of Christ through a new vocation: support of and participation in the crusade. Through their explanation of the crusade as an opportunity for personal identification with Christ and participation in the work of Christ, the crusade was clearly more than a war for the liberation of the Holy Land. It was a means of sanctifying the church as an "instrument for the moral transformation of the individual Christian and of Christian society as a whole."[10] One of the most important and well known crusade preachers, James of Vitry,[11] argues in his sermon *Precipit nobis Dominus*, that the "crusade stands as an outward sign of the internal acceptance of the cross in the hearts of the crusaders [. . .] For crusaders, the salvific action of the cross is dependent on true contrition and confession" and this conversion is equivalent to martyrdom which absolves them from every penalty of sin and secures for them eternal reward.[12]

In addition, wives and other relatives who share in the burdens of the crusade likewise share the same reward. Never before had the crusade been a means of sanctification for the entire body of believers. But now, raised to this level of a vocation available to all, not only was the work of the Church truly being accomplished through this activity, but the laity were for the first time on a par with monks, clergy and religious. Penance and conversion were placed in the forefront of the Church's agenda and everyone was asked to embrace it. Innocent's plan was carried to every corner of Christendom and responded to enthusiastically.

---

[10]Powell, *Anatomy of a Crusade* 63.

[11]For more on James of Vitry as a crusade preacher, and his negative attitude towards Muslims, see Hoeberichts, 32-41.

[12]Powell, *Anatomy of a Crusade* 55.

Attitudes Toward Muslims

Innocent rallied all the power of the Church behind his con-
demnation of the Saracens, using the Scriptures, the rationale
of the previous popes and his own passion for reclaiming the
Holy Land. His attitude towards and knowledge of the Saracens
was sadly very limited and all too common. Contemporary understandings about the culture, civilization and achievements
of the Muslim world were grossly inadequate, if not altogether
absent. *The Oxford History of Islam* states

> During the Middle Ages the West in general found it
> very difficult to formulate a coherent vision of Islam,
> constrained by its own narrow horizons as well as by a
> lack of sufficient and accurate information. For the most
> part Christians knew virtually nothing about the reli-
> gion of Islam, but saw the Saracens only as the enemy.[13]

Information about the Saracens that did exist came largely
through a few, limited sources. One was the *chansons de geste*, a
body of literature that chronicled among other things, the sup-
posed journey of Charlemagne to the East. Written during the
$11^{th} - 14^{th}$ centuries during the height of crusader fervor, these
songs glorified the heroic deeds of the Christians in the midst of
romance, chivalry and warfare. The descriptions of Islam were
wildly inaccurate, not even reflecting what was known at the
time. Underlying the songs was the theme that if the Saracens
could be defeated on the battlefield, they could be persuaded to
accept Christianity. The goal was the conversion of as many as
possible, not the extermination, of the enemy. On the positive
side, Saracen soldiers were portrayed as worthy enemies – brave
and noble – whose fault was the depraved religion they professed.[14] A second source of information originated from contemporary scholars, mostly Spanish. Although their material
also presented the violent and fanatical side of Islam, it was
generally well balanced and tried to portray Islam more realis-
tically than did the usual stereotypes which did Islam little, if

[13]Jane I. Smith, *The Oxford History of Islam* 321.
[14]Smith, *The Oxford History of Islam* 327.

any, justice. Returning crusaders supplied a third source – their own stories – which largely embellished their deeds while denigrating the Arab population. Regardless of even small attempts to portray Islam in any positive light, and in spite of their incredible achievements in art, architecture, literature, science and medicine, Muslims were generally considered to be uncivilized barbarians, condemned as heretics, despised as the enemy. A quick survey of writings which addressed this civilization shows an inadequate knowledge and lack of openness to this culture.[15]

One of the earliest persons to study and portray Islam was John of Damascus, a government official of the late 7th century who left his position to enter a Greek Orthodox monastery. Knowledgeable in Arabic and the doctrines of Islam, he wrote about what he called the heresy of Islam and of Muhammad as the Anti-Christ. Desiring Saracens and Christians to reason together, he also wrote about a debate between a Christian and Muslim, in which the Christian won. For being "Saracen-minded" and inclined toward the religion of Islam, he was condemned at the iconoclastic synod of 754.

Most Western Christian writings of the 9th and 10th centuries tended to be contemptuous and abusive of the Prophet Muhammad. A change of tone, however, is registered in the 12th century. Peter the Venerable (1092-1156), the renowned Abbot of Cluny, offered the most positive contribution to this discussion. Committed to a better understanding of Islam in order to combat it more intelligently, he commissioned the translation of the Qur'an and other Muslim texts which were gathered together into a body of literature known as the "Cluniac Corpus." With this Latin corpus, serious study of the Islamic religion really began. Until this time, most writing about Islam by Europeans had focused on Muhammad, who was portrayed "as an imposter, a licentious womanizer, an apostate Christian, a magician, and so on."[16] From England came three voices contrary

---

[15]Unless otherwise noted, the following information is summarized from *The Oxford History of Islam* 322-324.

[16]Richard C. Martin, *Islamic Studies: A History of Religions Approach*, 2nd ed. (Upper Saddle River, NJ: Prentice Hall, 1982) 36.

to the prevailing tone of the day: Isaac of Stella, the Cistercian philosopher and theologian, Walter Map and Ralph Niger. In general, these 12th century men objected to the use of violence and espoused the preaching of the faith as the true Christian approach to the Saracen heresy. Benjamin Kedar acknowledges that through the work of these three men, "none of whom was a leading figure" of his day, we at least know that in some learned circles there must have been discussion about the option of preaching Christianity to the Saracens rather than engaging them only on the battlefield.[17]

Before leaving the consideration of voices addressing the Muslim, we must make mention of Joachim of Fiore (1135-1202). Joachim, a Cistercian abbot who eventually founded his own community of reformed Cistercan monks, was considered by some, because of his writings on eschatology, to be a prophet.[18] Kedar tells us that Joachim was well informed about Islam and "dealt with the Saracens . . . within the framework of his eschatological view of history."[19] Joachim identified the Saracens

---

[17]Benjamin Z. Kedar, *Crusade and Mission: European Approaches toward the Muslim* (Princeton, Princeton University Press, 1984) 111-112. This trend continues into the 13th century. In his *Summa Contra Gentiles*, Thomas Aquinas (1225-1274) includes a polemic against Muhammad, but paid little attention to the religion of Islam. Finally, Raymond Llull (1235-1316) used the tactic of dialogical argumentation in the discussion of truths. Open to free discussion of the tenets of Islam and respectful of their tradition, the Christian (in Llull's writing) always "won" the argument. In addition to voluminous writings, he spent his life proposing (to Church and civil authorities) that language schools be established for those who would go to the Muslims. He earnestly promoted dialogue and conversation rather than the sword. Although tireless in his efforts, he made little impact on the approach of the Church towards the Muslims.

[18]Joachim believed that human history was comprised of three ages: the Old Testament, the New Testament and the coming Age of the Holy Spirit. This third age, he believed, was about to commence in the not-too-distant future, beginning with the appearance of the Anti-Christ and the corruption of the Church. This would consist of a peaceful Sabbath Age of the Holy Spirit which would be heralded by two new religious Orders who professed poverty and preached penance. These Orders would confront the Anti-Christ and reform the Church.

[19]Kedar, *Crusade and Mission* 113.

with the beast of the Apocalypse (13:3) and suggests that, while earlier crusades were necessary in the battle against the Anti-Christ, the New Age would now be inaugurated "by preaching more than by waging war."[20] Thus, for Joachim, a crusade at this time was no longer the means for winning back the Holy Land. Joachim believed "that a future crusade might enjoy divine support if the participants were to conquer their sins first. But he seems to have expected that spiritual action would once and for all eliminate the Saracen danger the crusade had only temporarily checked."[21] Joachim's was a minority voice. The vast majority of voices in the Church had since 1095 been swept up in the fervor of the anti-Islamic crusading movement. It would fall to other voices in the early 13th century to pick up the banner of peace. Francis of Assisi would be one such voice.

---

[20]Kedar, *Crusade and Mission* 115.
[21]Kedar, *Crusade and Mission* 116.

Chapter II

Francis' Two Encounters: With the Crusaders and the Sultan

Francis' Desire to Go to the Saracens

Innocent called all of Christendom to be involved in the Fifth Crusade. Curiously, as Hoeberichts reminds us, "no trace of his call can be found in the writings of Francis and his first brothers."[1] Neither, apparently, were they influenced by the decrees of the Fourth Lateran Council nor the letters of Pope Honorius. Hoeberichts continues:

> This forms a striking contrast with the decrees of the same Council and of Honorius III with regard to the eucharist and other matters. For even though we cannot find any literal quotation of a conciliar text in the *Regula non bullata*, the influence of the Council on the text of the Rule can be established in various places, especially in the first verse of chapter 17 on the permission to preach, and in chapters 18-20, on such diverse topics as the yearly chapter, orthodoxy, penance and the reception of the eucharist.

[1]Hoeberichts, *Francis and Islam* 4.

In a similar way the clear influence of the Council and the encyclical *Sane cum olim*[2] of Honorius III can be seen in Francis' letters.[3] "Evidently," states Hoeberichts, "Francis was selective with regard to papal documents."[4] While he heard the call to promote reverence for the eucharist, he appears not to have heard the call to support the crusades. What are we to make of this curious silence? It seems as though Francis did not give in to the moral pressure on the part of the authorities and did not accept the position that the crusades provided a means of salvation for the people. Nor did he join the chorus to propagandize for the crusades.

> Thus Francis occupied an exceptional position among his contemporaries with regard to the crusades and the attitude they expressed towards the Saracens and Islam. This is all the more striking since virtually the entire church from high to low was committed to the crusade.[5]

Hoeberichts goes on to note that "a small, insignificant man from Assisi dared to oppose this church policy" and makes reference to the testimony of Thomas of Split. Thomas describes the powerful preaching of Francis in Bologna in 1222 on the feast of the Assumption: "throughout his discourse he spoke of the duty of putting an end to hatreds and of arranging a new treaty of peace."[6] Evidently it was obvious to people who listened that Francis had a different approach to solving the problems besieging the peoples of the world. But we must return to the Francis of an earlier time. So, let us recall the desires and choices of Francis in 1212.

Thomas of Celano tells us of Francis' attempted voyage in 1212: "In the sixth year of his conversion, burning with the de-

---

[2]November 22, 1219.

[3]The eucharistic emphasis in *The Letter to the Clergy, Letter to the Custodes* and *Letter to the Rulers* is especially marked.

[4]Hoeberichts, *Francis and Islam* 4.

[5]Hoeberichts, *Francis and Islam* 5.

[6]Marion A. Habig, ed., *St. Francis of Assisi, Writings and Early Biographies: English Omnibus of the Sources for the life of St. Francis* (Chicago: Franciscan Herald Press, 1973) 1601.

sire for holy martyrdom, he wished to take a ship to the region of Syria to preach the Christian faith and repentance to the Saracens and other unbelievers."[7] Having departed with a companion from Ancona, a storm blew their ship off-course and they landed in Dalmatia. Since it was late in the season, they decided to return to Italy. This first attempt to preach to the Saracens thus ended in failure. It is important to note that Francis set out for the Saracens prior to the formal launching of the crusade in 1215. Thus, his reason for going could not be connected with the crusader fervor which that cry elicited.

"Not too long after this," Celano continues, "he began to travel towards Morocco to preach the gospel of Christ to the Miramamolin and his retinue. He was so carried away with desire that he would sometimes leave behind his companion on the journey and hurry ahead, intoxicated in spirit, in order to carry out his purpose."[8] However, in Spain Francis became ill and was again forced to return to Italy without having encountered the Moors.

[7] *1C* 55. From Regis Armstrong et al., eds., *The Saint*, Vol. 1 of *Francis of Assisi, Early Documents* (New York: New City Press, 1999). Hereafter this volume will be referred to as FA:ED 1. All references from the sources regarding the life of Francis are taken from this series unless otherwise noted.

[8] *1C* 56. This journey likely occurred in 1213, possibly associated with the recent Christian victory at Las Navas de Tolosa.

Francis at Damietta[9] – In the Crusaders' Camp

We hear from Celano[10] that Francis finally made it to Syria "in the 13th year of his conversion." Traveling with Italian reinforcements for the crusade, Francis arrived with several other friars[11] at the port of Acre, the Christian port northwest of Jerusalem. Either the whole group or, more likely, Francis and a few companions proceeded from Acre to the crusader's camp in Damietta. John of Brienne, King of the Latin Kingdom of Jerusalem, was the military leader of the crusade. The spiritual leader of the crusade was Cardinal Pelagius. Once in the camp, the impending defeat of the crusaders became clear to Francis. Disturbed, he sought advice from Illuminato.[12] As Celano narrates it, Francis tells him: "If the battle happens on this day the Lord has shown me that it will not go well for the Christians. But if I say this, they will take me for a fool, and if I keep silent my conscience won't leave me alone. What do you think I should do?"[13] Encouraged by his brother to share his vision with the crusaders, Francis does so. For this he is mocked and his message ignored. When the battle is engaged on the following day

---

[9]Main sources for this account include the Franciscan sources: *1C* 20: 57, *2C* 4:30, *LMj* 9: 7-8, *LMj* 11: 3, Jordan of Giano, *XIIIth Century Chronicles* 10-14; extra-Franciscan sources include James of Vitry's *Letter VI* (1220) and his *Historia Occidentalis*, the writings of al-Kamil's spiritual advisor, Fakhr ad-din al-Farisi, and a *Crusader Chronicle* attributed to Ernoul. James Powell suggests that two incidents from this chapter of Francis' life need to be looked at together: his sermon to the crusaders and his visit with al-Kamil. The preaching and actions of Francis speak to an alternative to war as a means of conversion. Francis invites both the Christians and the Muslims to end the war by conversion to the will of God rather than continued bloodshed. (*Anatomy of a Crusade*, 159.) We will look at those two incidents in detail.

[10]*1C* 57.

[11]Friars Illuminato, Peter of Catania, Leonard and Barbaro and probably others. It seems that Elias and Caesar of Speyer were already in the Holy Land: Elias as provincial of Syria since the 1217 Chapter and Caesar, a preacher on the Fifth Crusade, who became a friar in 1218 or 1219 through his acquaintance with Elias.

[12]This information is missing from Celano's *First Life* of Francis, but is included in the *Second Life*.

[13]*2C* 30.

(August 29, 1219), the crusaders suffer heavy losses and are defeated.

A closer look at this event in the life of Francis is warranted, however. Celano's account telling of Francis' prediction about the battle on August 29 has traditionally been understood to be a sign of Francis' gift of prophecy indicating his holiness ("saintliness"). Indeed the pericope is placed by Celano within a section titled "Francis' Spirit of Prophecy." But might there not be more than a prophecy contained in Francis' preaching? Jan Hoeberichts and Michael Cusato, both relying on the work of James Powell, propose that Celano *is* presenting more than a prophecy of Francis in his prediction of the defeat of the Crusaders.[14] Hoeberichts explains that it would not have been improbable for Francis, while in the crusaders' camp, to have been involved in discussions which were circulating at the time, namely, *whether it* **was**, in fact, "God's will" to engage in the crusades against the Muslims. It seems that the theory (accepted) since the call of the First Crusade (which identified the crusades as the will of God) was beginning to be called into question, if ever so slightly.[15] This discussion was rooted in Bernard of Clairvaux's rallying cry in support of the crusades, based on 2 Cor. 6:2 – "now is the acceptable time, now is the day of salvation" – clearly connoting that it was God's will the crusades be waged to recover the land of Christ. This passage was nearly synonymous with crusade theology in that the wars became identified with God's will, for: "now [was indeed] the acceptable time, now [was indeed] the day of salvation."

[14]Hoeberichts 96-98; Cusato class lecture: "Early Movement," Nov. 20, 2001. J. Powell, "Francesco d'Assisi e la Quinta Crociata: una missione de pace," *Schede Medievali*, 4 (1983), 68-77.

[15]Hoeberichts (p. 96) states that following the failed Second Crusade "many people started asking whether they should not be somewhat more modest with regard to such affirmations." Those "affirmations" referred to the use of 2 Cor. 6:2 identifying this crusade as being a time acceptable to God. Hoeberichts goes on to say that neither Pope Innocent III nor Pope Honorius III agreed with those opinions which questioned in any way whether God's will was to engage in this type of battle against the Saracens.

Hoeberichts tells us that Celano, writing in 1247, uses Francis' prediction as an *exemplum* to his readers to emphasize the importance of not hardening their hearts against the will of God. For by doing such, they would lose the battle. Celano does not tackle the question about whether "the crusades are God's will at this time," but he does conclude this pericope with the advice to his readers: "Let the princes of the whole world take note of this, and let them know: it is not easy to fight against God, that is, against the will of the Lord. [. . .] If victory is to be expected from on high, then battles must be entrusted to the divine Spirit."[16] The fact that he frames the account in terms of "time" indicates he is evoking Bernard's rallying cry based on 2 Cor. 6:2.

Indeed, Celano seems to imply that Francis' preaching is intended to warn the crusaders that "now is **no longer** the acceptable time." It was **no longer** God's will to engage in bloodshed and devastation. Rather, the very idea of the crusading movement was a violation of the will of God. Celano does this by making use of 2 Cor. 8:5 ("it is not easy to fight against [. . .] the will of God"). Francis was clearly contradicting the major justification for the impending battle and the entire crusade. In doing so he is connecting with the anti-crusade current articulated most clearly as we have seen by Joachim de Fiore. Celano seems to confirm that this was Francis' position also by equating the defeat of the Christians with their opposition to the will of God (by not listening to Francis).[17] Thus, it seems clear to me based on the previous analysis, that Francis went to Egypt to actively oppose the crusades.[18]

[16]*2C* 30.

[17]Hoeberichts (p. 97), again citing Powell, concludes: "Celano's story gives the impression that Francis spoke about one particular battle which he would have liked delayed because [. . .] the right moment had not yet come to start the battle. In fact, however, Francis' sermon was not directed against one particular battle (*pugnam*) which the crusaders wanted to start [. . .] but was meant to forbid the crusade as such (*bellum*) and to announce its failure."

[18]Whether or not Francis went to Egypt to oppose the crusade is a debated issue. Among those contemporary writers who believe he did are: James Powell (*Anatomy of a Crusade*, 158), Francis De Beer (*Francis of Assisi Today*, 16), Giulio Basetti-Sani (*Muhammad and St. Francis*,

The Vision of Francis

Where does this radical departure from the popular belief of the day come from? How does Francis get drawn into this major historical event and what significance does it have? I believe it is of tremendous value to explore these questions, for that brings us into the heart of what Francis was all about and contains a message of grave importance for our world today.

Francis was impelled by a vision which motivated him and which captured the hearts and energies of those who followed him. That vision is rooted in the life-changing event of Francis' famous encounter with the leper, recorded in his *Testament*. Here, Francis himself confirms the importance of that experience. Through the grace of God, Francis was led "***among*** lepers"[19] and "what had seemed bitter" to Francis was changed to "sweetness." *Among the lepers*, Francis' eyes were opened, and he saw what it meant to be human, he knew what it was to look on the face of God. This deeply personal revelation by God was pure grace. Henceforth, Francis views *all* creation, *all* existence as indelibly marked with the presence of Christ. Francis recognized that God, in becoming flesh in the person of Jesus Christ, so profoundly shared our human condition that "even the decaying flesh of a leper served as a tabernacle of God's presence."[20] What a complete reversal of vision was this for Francis! This cardinal insight of Francis' life forever changed the way he would relate to his society, his church and his God. For Francis saw:

That ALL, without exception, are creatures of the same God,

That ALL, without exception, are offered the same grace of salvation,

---

43), Jan Hoeberichts (*Francis and Islam*, 98) and Michael Cusato. Gwénolé Jeusset (*God is Courtesy*) does not address it directly, however it seems he would agree. Among those who disagree, that is, believe Francis supported the crusades are Christopher Maier (*Preaching the Crusades*, 12-17) and Tomaz Mastnak (*Crusading Peace*, 185). Benjamin Kedar identifies evidence on both sides and concludes it is a "moot point," that it cannot really be determined (*Crusade and Mission*, 130).

[19]Emphasis mine. Test 2.

[20]These images are drawn from a class lecture given by Michael Cusato, September 25, 2001.

That ALL, without exception, are endowed with the same human dignity and the same inestimable value,

That ALL, without exception, are *fratres et sorores,* one to another.

Shortly after this experience, Francis tells us, he "delayed a little and left the world." Cusato states:

> In this encounter with the lepers, Francis discovered an evangelical truth which would form the very foundation of his spirituality and of the movement which would form around him – the insight of the universal fraternity of all creation under the same God. Once Francis had been given this crucial insight, he further came to recognize that everything which breaks the bonds of this fraternity (through willful ignorance, moral blindness, or acts of injustice) is what, for him, constitutes "sin."[21]

Thus begins his life of penance, a life as radical as the insight Francis had experienced and which unfolds throughout the rest of his life.

Consequence of this Vision of Universal Fraternity

Along with this vision came a complete upheaval in the values that Francis espoused. The consequence of this vision, of this radical insight as to the meaning of human life and the action of God on behalf of God's creation, led Francis to "leave the world" and "begin to do penance." Cusato identifies the two ways in which Francis "left the world." First, by abandoning the values which were in conflict with the Gospel. Secondly, by moving outside the city of Assisi where the brothers were free to establish an evangelical based world of their own. Thus, Cusato concludes, "belief in the universal fraternity of all creatures also led Francis and his followers to separate themselves consciously from everything that was a source of division between human

---

[21]Michael Cusato, "Hermitage or Marketplace?" *True Followers of Justice: Identity, Insertion, and Itinerancy among the Early Franciscans* Spirit and Life, ed. Elise Saggau, vol. 10 (St. Bonaventure: Franciscan Institute, 2000) 11.

beings. . . They decided to live as the poor, among the poor. Henceforth, they would be not only a community of *fratres* but also a
fraternity of *minores*."[22]

In discerning how they would live out the mission they had
been entrusted with by God, the brothers knew that they must
share the truth they had received. Through lives of humble service (in word and example) they would call others to "do penance" by: 1) changing the way they saw the world through a
willingness to see it through the eyes of the suffering and ne-
glected and 2) changing the way they lived in the world, by using the goods of creation in such a way that everyone might
have what they need to live. Thus, the early Franciscan movement, rooted in the radical following of Jesus, embracing his
unconditional love and acceptance of each person, presented a
challenge to the existing religious and political structures of
the day. The inequality between the "haves" and "have-nots" in
the society at this time cannot be overestimated. Tremendous
gaps existed between those "with power" (money, land, posses-
sions, prestige) and those "without power." The complexities and
injustices of the emerging new monied economy resulted in severe suffering for a large part of the population who were basi-
cally invisible and discounted. It was this situation that Francis
and the early brothers first addressed by their radical stance.
The life of penance that Francis proposed asked nothing less
than being able to see God in "the other," to recognize their in-
nate dignity, indeed, to see in "the other" one's own brother or
sister. Surely this included the rights of all then to enjoy the
goods of creation. It was this "life of penance" (a life of relationship, a re-ordered societal structure) that would be able to heal
the divisions within the human fraternity.

This way of living (that is, a life of penance) is nothing less for
Francis than surrender to God's will. It is allowing oneself to be
directed by God's grace and holy activity. It demands conversion. And the point is to live a life of penance, a life in union
with God. This can result in nothing less than living God's own
life, which is communal, Trinitarian. Thus, communal (frater-

[22]Cusato, "Hermitage or Marketplace?" 12-13.

nal) life must be the result of penance, for penance leads us to God, thereby necessarily connecting us with the other. This is what Francis saw in Jesus, embraced as his own, and what is at the heart of the Franciscan way of life.[23] Part of Francis' total surrender to God is his embrace of poverty, which was how he saw Christ express his love. By total surrender ("emptying himself," Gethsemane, Calvary) to the will of the Father, Jesus perfectly lives out the command of love and thus accomplishes our redemption. Francis desires nothing other than embodying that same love, and living it in the manner of Jesus Christ, in order to thank, praise, honor, and bless the God who has emptied Godself for love of God's children. Thus poverty, for Francis, is both a material and spiritual reality. It is spiritual in that he freely gives up his own will in order to submit to the will of God. It is material in that, in union with the will of God who desires a universal fraternity among God's creation, all goods must be shared and each person must receive what they need and deserve. Thus, we return to the social implication of Francis' vision and way of life: living in and for God demands living as brother and sister to all, loving each as God loves each. As long as there were people in need, Francis desired only to give to them what they needed, as a caring brother would do. He desired to live the love of Christ. He also saw in their need the needy, humble, vulnerable God who lives in each person. It was Francis' image of God that defined Francis' vocation and mission.

The first consequence of the leper experience for Francis was that he embraced a life of penance. The second had to do with his image of God. Seeing Christ in his brothers and sisters, the lepers, Francis became overwhelmed at the extravagant love of God and the lengths to which God went in order to restore God's people to the fullness of life for which they were created. Truly, the Suffering Servant of Isaiah spoke to Francis who knew now of God's endless, unconditional and profound love for the human family. Francis understood the message of the Gospel and the depths of God's love as poured out in the life of Jesus. His

---

[23]This paragraph and the next relies on notes taken from Michael Blastic's class lecture of March 8, 2002.

appreciation for the absolute, selfless love of Jesus offered by his humble birth, life and passion, his death and resurrection knew no bounds. He yearned to be united with this God and to give himself to God's mission: the realization of the Kingdom of God through loving service after the manner of Jesus Christ. As Francis prayed before the crucifix, struck by the utter humility of such total surrender and unconditional love, he prayed:

Most High, glorious God,
Enlighten the darkness of my heart
And give me true faith, certain hope, and perfect charity,
Sense and knowledge,
Lord that I may carry out Your holy and true command.[24]

His only desire was to know God's will and carry it out. The God Francis worshiped was both "Most High and glorious" as well as the humble, suffering servant, born in a stable, shamefully executed on a cross. This was the God Francis was immersed in and to whom he gave his all. Nothing brought greater life or joy to Francis than doing God's will; than total surrender to God. Francis, at first alone and then with the brothers who joined him, discovered over and over, a confirmation of God's will in the Scriptures. Seeking to be directed by the Spirit of God they embraced the mission given them: to announce peace to the people and penance for the remission of sin.[25] From the very beginning, peace was connected to penance (living in relationship). This vocation and mission only deepens in his experience and articulation in the succeeding years. Moved by this truth, the vision of universal fraternity, Francis could never have bought into the crusades as a means for reclaiming the Holy Land, the land of God's Only Son, the Prince of Peace.

The Early Rule: Chapter 22: 1-4

Another clue to the reason for Francis' different and unpopular message to the crusaders is found in his *Early Rule* (22:1-4).

---

[24]*FA:ED* 1, 40.
[25]*1C* 23-29.

All my brothers: let us pay attention to what the Lord
says: Love your enemies and do good to those who hate
you for our Lord Jesus Christ, Whose footprints we must
follow, called His betrayer a friend and willingly offered
Himself to His executioners. Our friends, therefore, are
all those who unjustly inflict upon us distress and anguish, shame and injury, sorrow and punishment, martyrdom and death. We must love them greatly for we
shall possess eternal life because of what they bring us.[26]

What light could this shed on Francis' message to the crusaders about a new way to engage the Saracens? What might Francis
be saying in this passage?

Certain contemporary scholars see this chapter as a "testament" which Francis left his followers prior to his departure for
the Middle East in 1219.[27] Knowing full well that he might not
return from this journey,[28] it seems conceivable that Francis
would want to leave a final message to his brothers. Conscious
that he was headed into the territory of the "enemy," Francis
shares a very pointed, concise directive. It is a command: "let us
pay attention to what the Lord says: Love your enemies and do
good to those who hate you [. . .]." As we have seen, the Saracens
are generally known as "the enemy," "the infidel," as those who
wished the Christians no good: in short "those who hate" us.
Like in the beginning of *The First Letter to the Faithful*, Francis
recalls Jesus' command to love, a central truth for Francis.[29] He

[26]*FA:ED* 1, 79.

[27]Notably among these scholars are Flood, De Beer and Cusato. Flood
sees all of Chapter 22 as a Testament. Cusato, however, believes only
vv 1-4 report a farewell message. The rest he attributes to Francis'
resignation speech at the fall Chapter of 1220.

[28]Much discussion has centered on whether or not Francis went to
the Holy Land seeking martyrdom. Contemporary writers such as
Kedar, Powell, and Mastnak believe that martyrdom was sought by
Francis. Hoeberichts and De Beer disagree. While Francis' contem-
porary biographers identify this as a motive, the non-Franciscan sources,
James of Vitry and Ernoul, do not mention martyrdom. I do not believe
Francis was motivated by that desire.

[29]It is also interesting to note that both chapter 1 of *1LtF* and chapter
22 of *ER* end with verses from chapter 17 of John's Gospel, the High
Priestly Prayer of Christ: praying for those who are "sent into the world:
that they might be one, as we are one" among others.

goes further by specifying Jesus' ultimate acceptance and love of Judas by calling the one who is to betray him ("His betrayer"), a "friend." Then we hear of Jesus' surrender to the will of God: he who "willingly offered Himself to His executioners." The text next identifies who "our friends" are: "all those who unjustly inflict upon us distress and anguish, shame and injury, sorrow and punishment, martyrdom and death. We must love them greatly for we shall possess eternal life because of what they bring us."

In light of his vision of universal fraternity, it seems that these understandings of Francis could very well have been exactly what he wanted to leave his brothers as a way of summing up the core reality of his vision and the very heart of their movement. If he were not to return, these words would certainly be consoling for the brothers. More importantly, they emphatically present a call to live in the "footprints of Jesus": unconditional love even in the face of betrayal and forgiveness no matter how severe or terrible a treatment might have been suffered. This was the way of an authentic *frater minor*. Thus, what Francis is proposing is a complete reversal of the understanding of who our "friend" is – for the friend is also the one who injures us, brings about sorrow or even death. Because of that friend, *eternal life* comes to us! If these were the words of Francis to his brothers before he left for the East, not only would they help to console his brothers in the event of his death, they would also confirm once again the vision which was at the heart of their movement: to love everyone, even the "enemy," for that was the way of Jesus and thus must be the way of the Friars Minor. It seems that Francis, willing to undergo death at the hands of the Saracens, could very well have wanted that sacrifice to be an occasion of deepening the commitment to a Gospel presence (true fraternity) in the world. That call to peace and penance, the only way to restore the universal fraternity, was the only way to live in the world and was a clear renunciation of the continued violence of the crusades which could only further sever the bonds of the human family.

Understood in this light, Francis was clearly aware of the Saracens as his brothers and sisters and not as his enemies. He went to speak with them as brother to brother and not as "con-

queror" or "possessor of the truth." He went to see the face of
God in an unexpected place, just as he had experienced years
before in his encounter with the lepers. Francis had given his
life now, for thirteen years, to preaching penance, forgiveness,
peace and God's love. His desire now was to take that message,
in deed and in word, to his brothers and sisters, the Saracens.
Indeed, this was his third attempt to reach them. If this passage *was* written prior to his departure, as I believe it was, we
have a clear appreciation of how deeply imbedded in the heart
of Francis this vision of universal fraternity was. As we will see,
it will continue to grow deeper.

Thus it was that Francis went among the Saracens – with an
attitude, a vision and an expectation vastly different from – indeed, one opposed to – that of the Church. Francis went as a
friend into the camp of the 'enemy,' as a sheep among the wolves.
He approaches them as a brother, sent by God with the message
of repentance and salvation which he found most fully revealed
in Jesus Christ. But Francis' first message was his demeanor,
his stance: one of respect, courtesy and openness.

At Damietta — In the Sultan's Court

Jan Hoeberichts relies on the accounts of the chroniclers,
Ernoul and Bernard the Treasurer, in presenting Francis' and
Illuminato's courageous sojourn into the Muslim camp.[30] He
relates that after the defeat of the crusaders, the Sultan sent
one of the crusader prisoners back to the Christian camp with
an offer for a truce. This provided the opportunity for Francis to
carry out the rest of his mission. Francis requested permission
from Pelagius to go to the Sultan, which was, at first, denied.
After repeated requests, Pelagius finally gave in. Francis, accompanied by Brother Illuminato, went into the Saracen camp.
They were apprehended and beaten, then taken to the Sultan.
The Muslims may have thought that Francis and Illuminato
were carrying a response to the negotiations and thus brought

---

[30]Hoebericts, *Francis and Islam* 58-59. The thirteenth century
accounts of both Ernoul and Bernard represent "continuations" of the
famous late twelfth century Chronicle of William of Tyre of the crusades.

them to the Sultan. Sultan Malek-al-Kamil asks the two if they had brought a message or if they desired to convert to Islam. Francis replied that they were indeed messengers, coming not with a message from Cardinal Pelagius, however, but "with a message of the Lord God" (Ernoul), "as ambassadors of Our Lord Jesus Christ" (Bernard).[31] James of Vitry continues the story:

> When that cruel beast saw Francis, he recognized him as a man of God and changed his attitude into one of gentleness, and for some days he listened very attentively to Francis as he preached the faith of Christ to him and his followers. But ultimately, fearing that some of his soldiers would be converted to the Lord by the efficacy of his words and pass over to the Christian army, he ordered that Francis be returned to our camp with all reverence and security. At the end he said to Francis: "Pray for me, that God may deign to reveal to me the law and the faith which is more pleasing to Him.[32]

We know that Francis dialogued with the Sultan and his advisers for some time in an atmosphere that was conducive to exchanging the truths of each religion; invitations to conversion were also extended. Francis apparently never insults the Prophet nor denigrates the religion of Islam. He presents a case for Christ as the full revelation of God and Christianity as its fullest expression.[33] At the end of the discussion, Francis and

[31]Hoeberichts, *Francis and Islam* 58. Bonaventure tells us: "When that ruler inquired by whom, why, and how they had been sent and how they got there, Christ's servant, Francis, answered with an intrepid heart that he had been sent not by man but by the Most High God in order to point out to him and his people the way of salvation and to announce the Gospel of truth" *LMj* 9:8. Powell also relates this version of the account and adds "Obviously, Francis saw in conversion the means to peace and reconciliation" (*Anatomy of a Crusade*, 159).

[32]James of Vitry, *Historia occidentalis*, in *FA:ED* 1, 584.

[33]"Francis did not present a yes or no, true or false, faithful or treacherous alternative to him, forcing a manichean choice. The sultan understood that Francis respected his religion, even if Francis told him, from his point of view, that the Christian way was more pleasing to God. The sultan was struck by this mixture of conviction and tolerance ..." (F. De Beer, *We Saw Brother Francis*, trans. Maggi Despot and Paul Lachance [Chicago: Franciscan Herald Press, 1983] 77).

Illuminato were escorted, with gifts and guards, safely back to the crusaders' camp. Golubovich suggests that since fighting between the two armies resumed on September 26, the encounter between al-Kamil and Francis likely occurred between September 1 and 26.[34] It appears that Francis and al-Kamil spent a considerable amount of time exchanging religious views with each other. The next chapter of this paper will examine more carefully what some of those areas of discussion might have been.

Like Francis, the Sultan Malek al-Kamil was a man who desired peace.[35] This ruler had a reputation for kindness and fairness. The French Franciscan scholar of Christian-Islamic dialogue, Gwénolé Jeusset confirms this with the following:

> Once the decision [of surrender] was agreed upon, [al-Kamil] applies with humanity and courtesy which won the admiration of our chroniclers. Jean de Brienne, with noble resignation, had accepted to serve as hostage for the evacuation of Damiette. El-Kamil welcomed him as a king "showering him with marks of esteem such as he had never afforded to anyone." In a splendid tent on a high mound which dominated the theatre of operations, [. . .] he offered the knightly king a magnificent feast. But in the midst of the most flattering attentions the

[34]Girolamo Golubovich, *Biblioteca bio-bibliographia della Terra Santa e dell'Oriente Francescano,* (Quaracchi: Collegio di S. Bonaventura 1906) 1: 94-95.

[35]During this one offensive, he offered peace to the Crusaders no less than five times. All were refused by Cardinal Pelagius, often against the expressed desires of John of Brienne. Al-Kamil was known as a kind, generous, fair ruler. Accounts of his humane treatment of the defeated Crusaders, prisoners of the Saracens, abound in accounts of James of Vitry, Oliver of Cologne and Ernoul. Indeed, as James Powell writes: "The final act [of the Christian surrender of Damietta] was carried out with great propriety. The sultan treated his hostages with the respect befitting their rank and arranged for food for the army..." (James Powell, *Anatomy of a Crusade*, 191). This is in striking contrast to the gruesome atrocities committed by the Crusaders against the Muslims when Damietta fell to the Crusaders in Nov. 1219. Al-Kamil's attempts to make peace with the Christians continued on through the 1220's, culminating with the treaty of peace in 1229 with Frederick II.

old soldier could not restrain his tears. The sultan was astonished: "Why do you weep?" He could not bear seeing a king crying. "I cannot help weeping," answered Brienne, "when I see down there these poor men that God had entrusted to me dying of hunger." [. . .] Malik al-Kamil, seized with compassion, had at once sent the necessary food to the French. . .[36]

Oliver of Cologne, a crusade preacher and later a bishop and cardinal, relates another impression of al-Kamil. This excerpt from a letter concerns the feeding of the 30,000 crusader prisoners dying of hunger:

May the Lord always increase your happiness, O Kamil, and may he lift from your heart the veil of shadows so that you may know the truth! I, your freed prisoner, your servant redeemed by the cross, I will never be ungrateful for your kindnesses. Never before have ever been cited such examples of goodness in regard to enemy prisoners. When the Lord permitted that we fall into your hands, we did not have the impression of being in the empire of a tyrant or a master, but under the authority of a father who has showered us with good deeds, has saved us in danger, has visited us in our trials and even supported our complaints. You cared for our sick; you have reached out energetically against those who made fun of us.... Truly, as a just title, you are called "Kamil" which means "perfect," for you govern wisely and by your virtue you surpass all the princes...[37]

This was a man interested in dialoguing with the fascinating monk, so humble, so courageous, so committed to his God. James of Vitry tells us that al-Kamil "listened to Francis attentively." Like Francis, al-Kamil found a "new kind of enemy" in this poor man. For one thing he discovered that:

---

[36]Jeusset, *God is Courtesy* trans. Carolyn Frederick (n.p., n.d.) 36. Jeusset is quoting from Rene Grousset, *The Epoch of the Crusades* (Paris: Edition de libraries de France, 1955) 245.

[37]Jeusset, *God is Courtesy* 37, quoted in translation from Basetti-Sani, *Mohammed et Saint Francois* (Ottawa: Commissariat of the Holy Land, 1959) 167.

Christians are not all men thirsty for the blood of believers! Malek is very intrigued by this monk. [. . .]
Francis seems to know the stumbling blocks between
Islam and Christianity. [. . .] The monk is affirmed as a
Christian and goes straight to the essentials and . . . is
heard. [. . .] Here we are at a rendezvous of courtesy:
the two protagonists by the grace of God do not fall into
polemics. The Sultan poses questions in a very favorable manner, and the monk responds explaining his
faith, without insulting the other and without a word
against the "Prophet of Islam." [. . .] One does not imitate Christ with hatred and scorn.[38]

Fareed Munir sheds light on the encounter between Francis
and al-Kamil from the Muslim perspective. He identifies al-
Kamil as a man committed to the directives of his faith. This
places peace in a prominent position for the Qur'an commands
Muslims to accept peace over war. It even commands peace to
be sought in the midst of war. With this as his guide, al-Kamil's
aim was to "establish a mission of peaceful coexistence with
Christians."[39] In fact, Munir goes on to tell us that so strongly
did Malek al-Kamil promote peace that he has a reputation in
Islamic history as the "Muslim who opposed those Muslims who
were in favor of the Fifth Crusade."[40] Munir surmises that this
peace-oriented Sultan recognized the "Muslim-like character of
St. Francis."[41] Munir speaks of the unique approach and response
Francis had as he encountered this "different religion" and those
who professed it. Rather than condemning, detesting or putting
himself above the Saracens he spoke with (the common response
of Christians), he expressed obvious respect for their beliefs. In
Muslim terms Munir identifies the common ground shared by
these two men: the centrality of God and humanity's worship of
God, the primacy of prayer in life (even contemplative prayer),

---

[38]Jeusset, *God is Courtesy* 23-24.

[39]Fareed Munir, "Prophet Mohammad of Arabia and St. Francis of
Assisi in the Spirituality of Mission," *Islam and Franciscanism: A
Dialogue* (St. Bonaventure: Franciscan Institute, 2000) 25-42.

[40]Munir 34.

[41]Munir 37.

and the conscious choice to remain "in the world" and live simple
lives for the sake of God.[42] Yes, Malek al-Kamil had truly met a
kindred spirit in Francis of Assisi; he, too, had found a new
brother.

Thus the interactions and dialogues proceed – perhaps for as
many as 25 days. During that time, five times a day, a muezzin
calls from his minaret, exhorting all to stop what they are doing
and pray. Francis is touched by their prayer and their faith in
God. Truly God is present in these people. Truly these are children of God, also redeemed by Christ's saving action, even if
they do not acknowledge Him. Truly these are brothers and sisters to Francis, deserving of his loving care. As Francis takes
his leave from the court of Malek al-Kamil, the Sultan makes a
request of him. Obviously impressed with Francis' goodness and
his desire for the Muslims to know the truth, al-Kamil asks
Francis to pray for him, that God would reveal to him the right
path. "[T]he sultan, the king of Egypt, secretly begged him to
pray to the Lord for him so that, by divine inspiration, he might
adhere to that religion which was more pleasing to God."[43]
Jeusset sees this as simply an extension of the daily prayer of
all Muslims – asking that God guide them on the good road.[44]

Francis De Beer interprets the request of the Sultan to Francis
as containing the ultimate meaning of this event. De Beer sees
Francis transcending the cloister of Christianity in this encounter. He hears Francis inviting the Sultan to do the same act of
transcending boundaries. But the Sultan is not yet ready. He
does ask for Francis' prayers that he will make the right choice.

> Everything is held in suspense! Finally, there are no con-
> querors or conquered. One attempts not to conquer an
> adversary but only to come to a mutual understanding
> of a higher truth.[. . .] Brother Elias, in the encyclical
> announcing his death, wrote that Francis had come "to

[42]Munir 37-38.
[43]Christopher Maier, *Preaching the Crusades*, 10. Quote from James
of Vitry, *Lettres*, ed. R.B.C. Huygens (Leiden 1960), 133.
[44]Jeusset, *God is Courtesy* 40.

prepare a new people for the Lord." Those new people are precisely the Saracens: 'For his name has been made known everywhere, and the distant isles have heard of him.' A dialogue was initiated which transcended all quarrels, discussions, and arguments. And no one could go any further: neither Francis nor the sultan. One must wait for the hour of the Spirit. And the suspense has lasted for centuries![45]

---

[45]Francis De Beer, *We Saw Brother Francis*, trans. Maggi Despot and Paul Lachance (Chicago: Franciscan Herald Press, 1983) 88.

Chapter III

Francis' Encounter with Islam

Beliefs of Islam which were introduced to Francis

As we have noted, Francis may have spent up to three weeks in the company of the Sultan and his advisors. Three weeks is a significant amount of time. Numerous sources relate that this was a courteous, respectful exchange. Indeed, so remarkable must have been this encounter – for both men – that even Muslim sources carried the story of the "monk" who addressed the Sultan during the Fifth Crusade. On the tomb of al-Fakhr al-Farisi, a mystic and adviser of the Sultan, one reads:

> He was a man of many well-known virtues. And his adventure with al-Malik al-Kamil, and that which happened to him because of the monk is well known.[1]

That "monk," of course, could be none other than Francis of Assisi. Henceforth, for all of history, this advisor of the Sultan

[1]A. Natali, "Gli Arabi e S. Francesco alle Crociate," *L'Italia francescana* 33 (1958): 159. An excerpt of the full inscription can be found in English in Martiniano Roncaglia, *St. Francis of Assisi and the Middle East*, 3rd ed., trans. Stephen A. Janto (Cairo: Franciscan Center of Oriental Studies, 1954) 26. Roncaglia's source is Ahmad Yusuf, *Turbat al-Fakhr al-Farisi*, Cairo 1922, 17-18.

would be known from the inscription on his tombstone as the one who was present during the conversations between the Sultan al-Kamil and Francis. The story must have circulated widely during this time. Although the specific contents of these exchanges were never documented by any of the direct participants, it is not too difficult to speculate on what might have been discussed. Knowing the fervor of Francis for delivering his message of the Gospel, and the zeal of the Muslim Sultan and his court for spreading their religion, the focus obviously had to do with the path to God. Indeed, our accounts do confirm this.

I believe at this point it behooves us to examine some of the basic beliefs of Islam which were possibly discussed during the exchange between Francis and Illuminato and al-Kamil and his advisors. Let's look at some of what might have resonated with Francis during these encounters.

Concept of God: ALLAH

Allah is the ultimate focus of all devotion in Islam. Belief in the unity of God (*tawhid*) is the core concept of Islam, and the necessity of obedience to God's will is the bedrock underlying all Islamic piety. The unimaginable majesty and sovereignty of Allah, his infiniteness, formlessness, and simultaneous transcendency and immanence is Islam's essential tenet. Thus, the central act of *salat*, the ritual prayer, prescribes complete prostration before God, symbolizing complete obedience to the Creator and ruler of the universe.[2]

The centrality of Allah is absolutely essential to every dimension of life for the Muslims. At the heart of Islam is the *shahada*, their profession of faith: "There is no God but Allah and Muhammad is the Messenger [or Prophet] of God." Islam affirms a radical monotheism in which the doctrine of the oneness of God is central. Muslims believe that Allah is the creator and sustainer of the universe. Allah is all-merciful, all-loving, all-powerful, all-knowing, and present everywhere. Allah is the one who gives life and takes it back. Creation enjoys the gift of

[2]Azim A. Nanji, ed., *The Muslim Almanac* (NY: Gale Research Inc., 1996) 224.

free will. Humans are to be obedient to Allah but are not co-
erced into submission. Surrender to Allah's will brings freedom,
not slavery. No one exemplifies this surrender better than the
prophet Abraham. He shows what it means to place Allah first
in one's life, overcoming the temptation to idolatry to which
humans are so susceptible. John Renard explains:

> The Qur'an has Abraham say the words every Muslim
> says at the start of the ritual prayer as they face Mecca:
> "I have turned my face toward Him who created heav-
> ens and earth [i.e., not to created nature itself], as a
> seeker after the One God, in grateful surrender [liter-
> ally as a *hanif* and a *muslim*], and I worship none but
> God" (Qur'an 6:76-79). Abraham could face the true cen-
> ter of life only after he had eliminated all that could
> compete for his attention. Abraham was reading what
> the Qur'an calls the "signs on the horizons" for what
> they reveal of God. Speaking of those who reject that
> self-discipline, the Qur'an says (God speaking): "I will
> turn away from my signs those who walk proudly on
> earth. Though they see every sign, they will put no cre-
> dence in them. Though they may see the way of upright-
> ness they will not set out on it. Should they see the er-
> rant way, that they will claim as theirs; for they denied
> and refused to attend to our signs" (Qur'an 7:146).[3]

This unequivocal allegiance to God in such a way as to have
all relationships and priorities in order, is at the core of the terms
islam and *muslim*. S – L – M (related to the Hebrew *shalom*)
connotes wholeness and balance. "The word *islam* means 'submission,' but its three-letter root – *slm* – is the same as the
linguistic root of the word 'peace.' The inference here is that one
finds peace through submission to the will of God."[4] John Renard
explains: "When a person pursues that state in relation to God,

[3]John Renard, *Responses to 101 Questions on Islam* (Mahwah: Paulist
Press, 1998) 33.

[4]Karima Diane Alavi, "Turning to the Islamic Faith," *America*, March
4, 2002: 20. Islam is the infinitive of the stem *salima*, 'to be safe,' 'to be
secure.' "In its third form (*salama*), it signifies 'to make peace' or 'to
become at peace,' i.e. to be reconciled. In its fourth form (*aslama*), the
infinitive of which is *islam*, it acquires the sense of 'to resign,' 'to submit

it means attributing to God and to none else what belongs to God. [...] One who achieves that state of propriety in relation to God is a *muSLiM*; literally, 'one brings about a state of *SaLaM*' by acknowledging that God alone" is the only God.[5]

> Muslims believe that God has, since the beginning of time, actively communicated with and through all creation in a variety of ways. Foremost, God communicates in the very act of creating, by suffusing the universe with divine signs. More intimately, God communes with each animated being by infusing those same signs into every individual. God has established, moreover, a history of revelatory communication embodied in a succession of prophets, beginning with Adam. Through that unbroken chain of spokespersons, God has continued his self-revelation through another sign, namely, that of the verses of the scriptures given to the principal prophetic intermediaries.[6]

The most significant of the prophets are Moses, David, Jesus and Muhammad. Signs are very important to the Muslims and they include verses from scripture (*ayat*), revelations in creation (known as "signs on the horizon"), and signs within an individual (as suggested by the title *ayatullah*, "sign of God.") Purity of heart allows the signs to be discerned in the innermost recesses of the self.

The popular prayer "The Ninety-Nine Most Beautiful Names of God" offers an understanding of "Allah." These Names are taken from the Qur'an and recall the attributes by which God

oneself' or 'to surrender.' Hence Islam, in its ethico-religious significance, means 'the entire surrender to the will of God.' [...] Islam, as a principle of the law of God, is 'the manifesting of humility or submission, and outward conforming with the law of God, and the taking upon oneself to do or to say as the Prophet has done or said' ... coupled with 'a firm and internal belief of the heart.'" "Islam," *Catholic Encyclopedia*, ed. Gabriel Oussani, 9 Nov. 2001.

[5]Renard, *101 Questions on Islam* 36.

[6]Renard, *Seven Doors to Islam* (Berkeley: University of California Press, 1996) 2. An example of signs in creation from the Qur'an: "And how many a sign there is in the heavens and the earth which they pass on by, turning away!" (Chapter 12:105).

has made Godself known in revelation. The greatest of the names of God is the first one mentioned: Allah. This name refers "to the essence which unites all the attributes of divinity, so that none of them is left out, whereas each of the remaining names only refers to a single attribute. It is also the most specific of the names, since no one uses it for anyone other than Him."[7] The two most frequently invoked names are "Merciful" and "Gracious or Compassionate." The concept of mercy dominates the attributes of God and has a clear corollary in human behavior. A person participates in the mercy of God by showing mercy to those in need and by gentleness rather than violence, even to the extent of

> [. . .] regarding the disobedient with eyes of mercy and not contempt; letting every insubordination perpetrated in the world be as his own misfortune, [. . .] all out of mercy [. . .] His share in the name al-Rahim lies in not turning away from any needy persons without meeting their needs to the extent of his ability, not turning from any poor in his neighbourhood or town without commit-

[7]Al-Maqsad al-asna fi sharh asma'Allah al-husna, *Al-Ghazali: The Ninety-Nine Beautiful Names of God*, trans. David B. Burrell and Nazih Daher (Cambridge: The Islamic Texts Society, 1992) 51. Since I will address this again in reference to Francis' "Praises of God," a list of these 99 Names is found in Appendix 1. Muslims believe that the Names of God are actually countless, not limited to 99, which is a symbolic number. These names come from the authority of Abu Haurayra who said "God...has 99 names, and whoever enumerates them enters paradise." While these names contain the greatest name of God, they also hide it. Yet it is said: "The supreme name of God is in the two verses *Your God is One God; there is no God save Him, the Infinitely Good, the Merciful* (II:163), and the beginning of the sura *Family of 'Imran: there is no God save Him, the Living, the Eternal* (III:1-2) 173. The second name of God is Al-Rahman (The Infinitely Good), followed by the third, Al-Rahim (The Merciful). Both of these are derived from Mercy. "Al-Rahman is more specific than Al-Rahim, in that no one except God . . . is named by it, whereas Al-Rahim may be used for others. [. . .] The Infinitely Good is He who loves men, first by creating them; second, by guiding them to faith and to the means of salvation; third, by making them happy in the next world; and fourth, by granting them the contemplation of His noble face" (Al-Maqsad al-asna fi sharh asma'Allah al-husna, *Al-Ghazali: The Ninety-Nine Beautiful Names of God* 54).

ting himself to them and ridding them of their poverty
– either from his own wealth or reputation, or by inter-
ceding on their behalf with another. And if he be unable
to do all that, he should assist them by prayer or by
showing grief on account of their need, in sympathy and
love towards them, as though he were thereby sharing
in their misfortune and their need.[8]

All but one of the 114 chapters of the Qur'an begin with the
phrase: "in the name of God, the Compassionate and Merciful..."
Renard tells us, "Not one of the Ninety-Nine Names of God, on
which they meditate as they finger the thirty-three beads of the
[subha,] will sound a dissonant note in the ear of Christian or
Jew."[9] The Ninety-Nine names encompass both the approach-
able/beautiful attributes of God and God's divine majesty and
awe-inspiring power. Thus, both the immanence and the transcendence of God is acknowledged.

In summing up the Muslim theology of the Ninety-Nine Beautiful Names of God, it is to be noted:

> There are but 99 names by which God . . . has named
> Himself, and they do not reach 100 because, 'He is odd
> [i.e., one] and loves what is odd.' Furthermore, 'the Lov-
> ing' and 'the Benefactor' and those like them are included
> in their total. But a knowledge of the totality of them is
> not possible short of an inquiry into the book [Qur'an]
> and the tradition [Sunna], since many of them are con-
> firmed in the book of God. . . and many of them are in
> the accounts of hadith as well.[10]

The Qur'an is the Holy Book of Islam, considered to be the
actual word of God, dictated directly to Muhammad.[11] The sa-
credness and prominence of the Qur'an cannot be overstated.

---

[8]Al-Maqsad al-asna fi sharh asma'Allah al-husna, *Al-Ghazali: The
Ninety-Nine Beautiful Names of God*, 54-55.

[9]Renard, *101 Questions on Islam* 37.

[10]Al-Maqsad al-asna fi sharh asma'Allah al-husna, *Al-Ghazali: The
Ninety-Nine Beautiful Names of God*, 175.

[11]Just as for Christians, Jesus is the presence of God in the world
(continually present in the Eucharist, the Word, the Assembly), for
Muslims the presence of God is the Qur'an.

Seeing phrases from the Qur'an (recall the ornate decoration on Islamic buildings with the beautiful caligraphied Qur'anic verses[12]) and hearing it recited are essential aspects of Islamic life. A sense of awe and humility accompanied by deep feeling are the hallmarks of listening to the scripture or of reciting it. To pronounce the Qur'an devoutly is to have the Word on one's tongue and thus to receive it most profoundly. To gaze upon the beauty of God's word brings pure delight. "For Muslims [. . .] the words of God and Muhammad are a living presence, an atmosphere as pervasive as the air they breathe."[13]

Prayer: *Salat*

The primacy of God in the lives of the Muslims is experienced most deeply in their prayer life. The primary function of prayer is the personal communication with God for the purpose of maintaining the abiding presence of God in every aspect of life. Five times each day Muslims are called by the muezzin to turn towards Mecca and pray. This disciplined rhythm gives structure to the day and fosters a sense of community and shared identity among Muslims. From minarets, the muezzin publicly announces the call to prayer, a dramatic gesture which dominates both day and night.

The Qur'an identifies numerous attitudes which Muslims are to embrace. Among the essential ones are attentiveness, intention, striving and gratitude. Prayer has a special place in teaching these attitudes. "Attentiveness means seeing things as they really are, with the eyes of faith; it means discerning in creation and in oneself, as well as in the revealed scripture, the signs of the Creator and Redeemer."[14] Right intention must precede all

---

[12]"Epigraphy includes the application of inscriptions to building, tombstones, mosque lamps, prayer carpets and a wide variety of other objects whose content is religious or whose function is sacred. [. . .] Some structures, such as the Taj Mahal, exhibit epigraphic programs of such intricacy as to remind one of the sculptural and stained-glass iconographic arrangements of cathedrals like Chartres and Notre Dame." (Renard, *Seven Doors to Islam* 27.)

[13]Renard, *Seven Doors to Islam* 27

[14]Renard, *Seven Doors to Islam* 10.

just acts and is part of the purification ritual before the prayer. It combines 'full awareness' of the heart with a single-heartedness towards God to desire God fully.[15] The greatly misunderstood Islamic theme of striving, *jihad*, lies at the center of the human condition and is essential in overcoming the ego in order to live for God. It is therefore first and foremost a posture of prayerfulness. Because of its importance, *jihad* will be treated more extensively later in this paper. Forgiveness is mentioned often in the Qur'an and is also a major focus of prayer. Equally important in shaping one's actions is gratitude.

> All positive virtues flow from the awareness that God is the beneficent and unstinting source of all good, who expects that those most blessed will in turn share their gifts most generously with others. To attain the experience of gratitude, one must be purified of any delusions of grandeur or self-sufficiency, as well as of selfish motivation in giving. The term that came to mean "almsgiving," derives from a root meaning "to purify oneself."[16]

Gratitude can do nothing other than overflow into praise of God. This praise which is gratitude, takes the form both of verbal prayer (as in the Ninety-Nine Names of God) and of generosity towards those in need. Social responsibility is a very serious obligation in Islam. Those who hoard their wealth are condemned by the Qur'an as are "those who do not treat the orphan with dignity nor encourage each other to feed the poor...[and who] greedily devour their inheritances" (Qur'an 89:17-19).[17]

Mercy, compassion, forgiveness, and pardon are among the most frequently acknowledged attributes of God and most prayed for spiritual gifts. God's infinite patience longs to grant forgiveness and calls people to repentance, that is, to "turn around." Forgiveness is as important in human relationships as it is with God. Muhammad is an example of one who constantly sought

---

[15]For an example of this, see Appendix 2.
[16]Renard, *Seven Doors to Islam* 11.
[17]Renard, *Seven Doors to Islam* 12.

God's forgiveness[18] and who was always ready to forgive. Related to the centrality of forgiveness in Islam is the concept of peace, which comes through submission to God's will. The very gestures and rituals of the "*salat*" express peace and submission. The Qur'an states: "The true servants of the All-Merciful are only those who walk humbly on the earth and who, when the ignorant address them, reply with words of peace" (25: 63). The word "*salat*" shares its linguistic root with the word for "connection." As Muslims put their faces to the ground in an act of submission to God, they practice the "Remembrance of Allah" and are "reminded that when their connection to God is broken, the world tumbles into a darkened chaos."[19] This connection to God also speaks to relations with others, particularly those who are considered enemies: "[H]old fast all together by the rope which Allah [stretches out for you] and be not divided among yourselves; and remember with gratitude Allah's favor on you; for ye were enemies and He joined your hearts in love so that by His grace ye became brethren..." (Qur'an 3:103).

Remembrance and mindfulness (or recollection) is a specific form of Islamic prayer known as *dhikr*. It is a prayer of simple praise and acknowledgement of God's sovereignty without any request or petition.[20] Ghazali recommends *dhikr* as a constant practice, an ongoing way of being before God.[21] This type of prayer fosters a presence of the heart. Repeated words or phrases, such as invocations of God (The Ninety-Nine Names) are examples of this prayer. For Muslims, the entire body prays. The following, from John Renard, illuminates this concept:

> The *dhikr* of the eyes is weeping; the *dhikr* of the ears is listening; the *dhikr* of the tongues is praise and laud; the *dhikr* of the hands is distribution and giving; the

[18]Renard notes that a *hadith* recounts Mohammad as saying: "My heart is clouded until I have sought God's forgiveness 70 times day and night" (Renard, *Seven Doors to Islam* 71).

[19]Alavi, "Turning to the Islamic Faith" 20.

[20]In one story from the *hadith*, Muhammad is asked what is most meritorious. He replies "to die while your tongue is moistened" with the remembrance of God.

[21]Renard, *Seven Doors to Islam* 54.

dhikr of the body is effort and accomplishment; the *dhikr*
of the heart is fear and hope, and the *dhikr* of the spirit
is surrender and satisfaction in God.[22]

Dhikr eventually became associated with the Sufi orders which
we will now look at briefly.

Sufis

Sufism (*tariqa*) is the generally accepted name for mysticism
in Islam which traces its origins back to Muhammad. It was
always a communal rather than individual reality. Sufis lived
in community. They constituted a spiritual family. "A dervish
must never say 'my shoes' or 'my so-and-so' – he should have no
private property. If one possesses anything, he should give it to
the brethren; otherwise he will lose his spiritual rank. How can
one say 'mine' when he knows that everything belongs to God?"[23]

Both spiritual and social needs of some Muslims found their
resolution in Sufism. In its formative period,[24] Sufism was an
interiorization of Islam, a personal experience of Islam's central mystery: to declare that God is One. Throughout its history,
the quintessence of Sufism sought to express anew that "there
is no deity but Allah" and that he alone must be the object of
worship.[25] When the formal structure of Islam seemed to some
Muslims too static an environment within which to experience
God, small communities of Muslims began to gather around a
"holy person." In this new community, they sought deeper union
with God through a more personal experience of God. These
groups adopted a threefold attitude of *islam* (complete and exclusive surrender to God's will specifically as expressed in the

[22]Renard, *Seven Doors to Islam* 55.

[23]Annemarie Schimmel, *Mystical Dimensions of Islam* (Chapel Hill:
University of North Carolina Press, 1975) 230.

[24]By the end of the eighth century a woman from Baghdad named
Rabia, the first great mystical poet of the Sufis, began speaking of her
loving relationship with God. Within a century there were many more
such poets throughout the Middle East. Around these mystics and other
holy people small groups of seekers formed. Such were the roots of the
religious orders, including the Sufis. Renard, *101 Questions*, 75.

[25]Schimmel, *Mystical Dimensions of Islam* 17-23.

teaching of the Qur'an), *iman* (the "faith" which is the interiorizing of the truths) and *ihsan* (the worship of God as if one sees God). *Ihsan* is the only one not contained in the Qur'an, yet the Qur'an states "mercy is with those who practice *ihsan*." "With the addition of [*ihsan*] the complete interiorization of Islam begins; for the believer has to feel that he stands every moment in the presence of God, that he has to behave with awe and respect, and must never fall back into the 'sleep of heedlessness,' never forget the all-embracing divine presence."[26]

> The goal of the Sufi is to become so at one with God, that "me" is no longer even heard. This type of total commitment to God is possible through the necessary solitude and 'deprivation' of addictive habits of mind and body which may be obliterated through the eventual process of purification. Whether the internal desert or the pure mountain, the seeker is aiming to achieve a unity within, which is possible for one whose eyes remain on the vision of divine revelation.[27]

The institution of the Sufi order, is also rooted in a social response to developments in Islamic history. From the earliest days of conquest and empire, many Muslims felt that the acquisition of wealth and worldly gain had destroyed the possibility of one's living according to the Qur'an and the *Sunna*.[28] These Muslims preferred a life of asceticism, which expressed itself in a life of poverty for the sake of God. In their lives of strict renunciation of the world and what was in it:

> [They] relied on the Prophet's word: "If ye knew what I know ye would laugh little and weep much. Therefore they were known as "those who constantly weep, for both the miserable state of the world and the meditation of their own shortcomings made them cry in hope of di-

---

[26]Schimmel, *Mystical Dimensions of Islam* 29.

[27]Maria Jaoudi, *Christian and Islamic Spirituality: Sharing a Journey* (Mahwah: Paulist Press, 1993) 33.

[28]The *Sunna* is the example or practice of the Prophet Muhammad as reported by his companions. It is composed of Muhammad's deeds, utterances and unspoken approval. The *Sunna* is a source of authority in Islam second only to the Qur'an.

vine help and forgiveness. Ibn ar-Rumi, the Iraqi poet of the 9th century, attests that 'God is fond of His servant's crying.'"[29]

As Islam expanded into such regions as Africa and India, where other religious traditions were quite alien to the Qur'an and the *Sunna*, the exclusivist claims of *Sunni* and *Shi'i* Islam, requiring absolute conversion, set Islam over and against other traditions.[30] The more universalistic, inclusive, and encompassing qualities of Sufism proved to be more successful in bringing non-Muslims and the uneducated into contact with the literary demands of the Qur'an and the *Sunna*.[31]

There are numerous stories about Christians interacting with Muslims, usually for the purpose of explaining some mystical truth to a seeker. Annemarie Schimmel, quoting various Islamic sources, tells us:

> Jesus, the last prophet before Muhammad according to Koranic revelation, appears to the Sufis as the ideal ascetic and also as the pure lover of God. A homeless pilgrim, wandering without knowing where to put his head, he instructs the devout about the importance of modesty, peace, and charity, for "just as the seed does not grow but from dust, so the seed of wisdom does not grow but from a heart like dust." It is the Jesus of the Sermon on the Mount whose image is reflected in sayings of the first generations of Sufis, and he continued to be a favorite figure in later Sufi poetry as well: he and his virgin mother become exalted symbolic figures.[32]

[29]Schimmel, *Mystical Dimensions of Islam* 31.

[30]Following Muhammad's death (623), a series of caliphs ruled over the Muslim community, not without major divisions and power struggles. In the second half of the 8th century these differences resulted in the two main divisions of Islam: Shi'i (recognizing authority which comes from hereditary succession of the descendants of Muhammad) and Sunni (who believe that leadership of the community resides in the community at large). Today about 10 per cent of Muslims are Shi'i (Shi'a, Shi'ite) who live primarily in Iran, Iraq and Lebanon. Sunni's comprise the vast majority (90 per cent).

[31]Martin, *Islamic Studies* 238.

[32]Schimmel, *Mystical Dimensions of Islam* 34-35.

Schimmel goes on to suggest that it may even be possible that the Sufis adopted their garment from Christian ascetics. And Roncaglia elaborates: the word itself designates a "rough, woolen (*suf*) tunic bound with a cord." Many of the Sufis lived by begging, believing that a true Sufi was the "one who posseses nothing and is possessed by nothing."[33]

Sufi writers were prolific and wrote of their experiences of divine love and extraordinary levels of intimacy with God. Ad-Din Daya Razi's (d. 1256) *Path of [God's] Servants* was especially concerned with translating lofty principles of spirituality into everyday morality for ordinary people. Razi does not see "spiritual seekers" as a separate category of people. Rather he believes that all are called to explore God's intimate invitation to the fullest of their capacity and to follow the path that God opens up to them.[34] This was typical of the Sufi's vision of life. It seems that just as Sufis believed they must share whatever they had with those in need, they must also share with everyone the truth they possessed, that is, the way leading to salvation.

Roncaglia is among those who suggest that Francis might have appeared to the court of al-Kamil as one similar to their own "Sufis." He further suggests that the Sultan was attracted to Francis, "even permitting him to speak with great liberty, though his convictions remained unchanged." We are told that al-Kamil "had a passion for Sufi mystical poetry and especially for the works of the great 'Umar ibn-al-Farid (1181-1235), one of the finest Islamic writers on the very Franciscan subject of an intense personal love of God."[35] Indeed, al-Farisi, mentioned above, who served as al-Kamil's spiritual advisor, was himself a sufi.

Before leaving Sufism, we will look briefly at two of the more prominent Sufi mystics: Rabia (8th century) and Rumi (13th century). Rabia (c. 717-801) is the most famous woman Sufi. She is generally the one credited with introducing the element of selfless love into the austere teaching of the early Sufis and bring-

[33]M. Roncaglia, "S. Francesco d'Assisi in Oriente," *Studi francescani* 3a ser. 25 (1953) 101.

[34]Renard, *Seven Doors to Islam* 211.

[35]Omer Englebert, *Saint Francis of Assisi: A Biography* (Chicago: Franciscan Herald Press, 1965) 479.

ing true mysticism into the Sufi tradition. Rabia's experience of God was profound and totally encompassing. She meditated for extensive periods of time and developed specific spiritual exercises, ran her own home, and taught those who came to her for guidance. Many who desired a relationship of union with God, sought her out for advice and teaching. She experienced the presence of God in the created universe. Her reputation for relating to animals was widespread. "No animal ran from Rabia, [. . .] all the animals, the deer and the wild asses, the goats and gazelles, came up to her, and gazed at her, and danced around her." She declined a continuous flow of marriage proposals and never married. "Rabia is the herald of love mysticism in Sufism, her very clear prayer consisting of the words '[O Lord] Thou art enough for me.'" The sole focus for Rabia was hope in God and the word of God's praise.[36]

Jelalludin Rumi (1207-1273) was a scholar and lawyer who taught Quranic law. He was born in Afghanistan. When he was 37 years old he met a wandering dervish by the name of Shams. He left his teaching and became a student of Shams because, as he said: "What I had thought of before as God, I met today in a person." After Shams was murdered, Rumi lived the life of prayer and union with God to which Shams had introduced him. He is one of the best known Sufi poets of all time. His poetic imagery leads one to the deepest levels of mystical oneness. He held, with others, that true belief and love of God were able to transport one "beyond the boundaries of traditional communities of faith." This was not a rejection of Islam but an attempt to express the power of any authentic relationship with God. "God, they reasoned, is bigger than all of our petty divisions – including those our religious boundaries seem to create."[37] In this sense, Rumi, and other Sufis, articulated that no religious community is big enough to express the fullness of God. Rumi wrote exquisite mystical poetry about love and union with the divine, rooted in a personal experience of loss and grief, of relinquishment. It developed in discipline and the abandon of surrender.

[36]Material about Rabia is summarized from Jaoudi, 15-18. For an example of Rabia's prayers, see Appendix 2.

[37]Renard, *101 Questions on Islam* 77.

Jihad

In his exchange at the court of the Sultan, Malek al-Kamil, Francis may also have discussed the Islamic concept of *jihad*, which means to "strive" or to "struggle." 'Striving for moral and religious perfection' by striving to realize God's will is the general meaning of the term. It is understood, in its first meaning, in terms of exhausting one's effort in order to please God. It applies to leading a virtuous life, persevering toward what is right and good. At the same time, it is struggling against any forgetfulness of God. Islam teaches that the greatest enemy is within the person and is identified as "the *nafs* (ego): the part of us that is led by our greed and arrogance, rather than the inner-self that God created in order that it might worship him and bring a sense of balance, peace and justice to the world."[38] The *Oxford History of Islam* states:

> At the center of the human condition lies the need to struggle, to strive against one's baser tendencies and against the spiritual entropy born of the heedlessness that is endemic to the human race. This is the core of that most misunderstood of Islamic themes, jihad. The Arabic root *Ja-Ha-Da* . . . means "to exert oneself." Believers must struggle against whatever stands between the self and its origin and goal, and strive to overcome injustice and oppression.[39]

Thus, the greatest struggle one endures is a spiritual one: against one's own lower self (hence, the "Greater *Jihad*"). Because Islam regards itself as a universal religion, *jihad* can also be exercised in the service or the spread of, or defense of, Islam.[40] The "Lesser *Jihad*" is a military struggle conducted against infidels (one which can only be successful if it is preceded first by a personal spiritual struggle). Throughout the centuries, different types of *jihad* have been identified.

[38]Alavi, "Turning to the Islamic Faith" 18.
[39]Donner, *The Oxford History of Islam* 11.
[40]Martin, *Islamic Studies* 15.

1) Jihad of the heart, which leads the struggle against temptations and the evil within, in order to comply with God's will and be pure of heart,

2) Jihad of the tongue, which uses the power of speech for that which is good and denies that which is evil,

3) Jihad of the hand, which defends the weak from the oppressor and which works toward bringing about a just world,

4) Jihad of the sword, ("holy war") which is to be used only as a last resort in defense of Islam. This includes the use of political or diplomatic avenues.[41]

Even though the spiritual meaning of *jihad* is the deeper meaning and had three clearly defined peaceful expressions, it is the "holy war" understanding of *jihad* that is best known. This does an injustice to a central tenet of Islamic faith, which Abu-l-Abbas al-Sabti (d. 1204) described as: "the expenditure of oneself for the pleasure of God Most High, emptying oneself of everything for His sake, and divesting oneself of reliance on the material world."[42]

Common Ground: Francis

During his time in the Levant, particularly during his weeks in the tent of al-Kamil, Francis would have encountered some of the main tenets and practices of Islam. He would have heard of their **God**: the **One** and Only, God of Abraham, Moses and Jesus, Allah, whose primary attribute is Mercy, who created the world, is known through **signs** in the world, and who brings people who live according to his ways, at the end of their lives, home to enjoy life with God forever. He heard of the **reverence**

[41]Alavi, *"Turning to the Islamic Faith"* 18-19. The first three are known as the peaceful forms of *jihad.*

[42]Vincent J. Cornell, *Oxford History of Islam* 103. Cornell also tells us that al-Sabti is the "patron saint of Marrakesh and the North African equivalent of Mother Teresa or St. Francis of Assisi" (98). For further information see Roy Parviz Mottahedeh and Ridwan al-Sayyid, "The Idea of the Jihad in Islam before the Crusades," *The Crusades from the Perspective of Byzantium and the Muslim World* ed. Angeliki E. Laiou and Roy P Mottahedeh (Washington: Darbarton Oaks, 2001) 23-29.

they had for the **Name** of God. He heard of the presence of God on earth in **God's Word**, the Holy Qur'an. He experienced their **reverence** for this **Word** in their attentive listening, savoring the Word on their tongue, their respect for the written word (calligraphy) decorating their mosques. He experienced their receiving this Holy Word as a living presence among them. He heard about and witnessed their rich and pervasive **prayer life**: being called to prayer five times a day, complete with a **purification** ritual and **prostrations**.[43] This is a prayer of the heart in which the whole body participated. It acknowledged the **struggle involved in turning one's heart to God** and the constant temptation to turn to self in place of God. It recognized what a proper response **tears and weeping** is for the alienation from God humankind experiences. It celebrated **gratitude** to the giver of all good gifts in word and action, specifically through **generosity to the poor**. In its most **mystical form** it proclaims the rootedness of the human in God's love and desires nothing but **deeper union with that loving God**. Within that context, love is the way and the means and the goal unto **radical transformation** so that even the **enemy can become the friend**. In the striving to **surrender to God's will** and thus enter into **God's peace** (the true meaning of Islam/Muslim) one **empties oneself** of everything for God's sake and **divests** oneself of reliance on the material world. Thus, the struggle with oneself, if victorious, brings about **true freedom** to be exactly what God created the person to be, one who freely chooses to embrace God's ways/God's path of mercy and compassion. This brings about **unity** and **oneness** on the earth **among all peoples**, reflective of Allah who is One. No matter what others thought about the Saracens, Francis found them to be believing, praying, peace-filled people. No doubt the **greeting** so dear to Francis, "May the Lord give you peace" was well received in the court of the Sultan, even as their "**Assalam aleikum**" ("May the peace, mercy, and blessings of Allah be upon you" or, simply, "peace be with you") must have thrilled him.

---

[43]The word "mosque" means "prostration."

This is at least a portion of the reality of Islam Francis encountered in Damietta. It must have been awesome for him to
experience some things so contrary to the popular image of Islam circulating in his day. As Jan Hoeberichts says:

> He discovered God's presence there where, according to
> the preaching of the church, only lies could be found; he
> saw the faith of the Saracens and was profoundly im-
> pressed by their prayer while everyone else called them
> unbelievers, [. . .] he listened with great attention to all
> that God was telling him through the Saracens' lives
> and history, and while others looked down on them,
> Francis was full of admiration: God had gone among
> the Saracens before him and had been the source of much
> that was good and beautiful. And where people had
> warned him of a 'wolf,' 'a cruel beast,' Francis met a
> friend.[44]

How did Francis receive all this? With respect and courtesy,
just as he was received by the Sultan. Having learned a powerful lesson many years before through his encounter with the
leper, Francis went to the Saracens open to discovering a brother,
a friend, the face of God. He went open to learning new truths
about God. He went eager to share the Good News of Jesus with
the Saracens. He went as Jesus went, obedient, humble, peaceful. Because of his approach, he was well received. When it came
time for him to leave, as a good Christian Sufi Francis declined
the gifts offered by the Sultan although he likely did accept a
horn for calling people to prayer. It seems he also left marked
for the rest of his life with an imprint which would show itself
in a variety of ways. We will look at those in the next chapter.

[44]Hoeberichts, *Francis and Islam* 70.

Chapter IV

Was Francis Influenced by Islam?

Francis' Actions after Damietta

There is no documented information about Francis' departure from Damietta or the Holy Land. Some suggest that he was present when the Crusaders were victorious over the Muslims, capturing the city of Damietta (November 5, 1219). Whether he visited the Holy Places in Palestine is unknown, although speculation suggests that he would have.[1] During that time, Brother Stephen traveled from Italy to inform Francis of new troubles brewing in the Order.[2] Francis, accompanied by Brothers Illuminato, Peter, Elias, Caesar of Speyer and the others, returned to Italy. Our attention now shifts to events in the life of Francis after his encounter with the Sultan and how they may have been influenced by his experience in Egypt. Specifically,

---

[1]A chronology prepared by Omer Englebert and Raphael Brown for *St. Francis of Assisi, Writings and Early Biographies: English Omnibus of the Sources for the Life of St. Francis*, (Chicago: Franciscan Herald Press, 1973) xi – xiv, indicates that Francis goes to Acre and the Holy Land in early 1220. It further records that he returns to Italy, landing in Venice, in spring or summer, 1220.

[2]Jordan of Giano, *XIIIth Century Chronicles*, trans. Placid Hermann (Chicago: Franciscan Herald Press, 1961) 27.

we will look at Chapter 16 of the *Early Rule*, Francis' resignation, certain letters that he wrote, his experience on Mt. La Verna, and, finally, his *Canticle of the Creatures*.

Early Rule, Chapter 16

The dating of Chapter 16 of the *Early Rule* is, not surprisingly, inconclusive. While Anton Rotzetter holds that it was written prior to Francis' departure for the East (he suggests that it is a logical consequence of the earlier chapters and actually written as an alternative to the crusades), Walbert Buhlmann posits that it would not have been possible for Francis to write it without his personal experience among the Saracens. Leonhard Lehmann, having held the former position, now agrees with Buhlmann.[3] David Flood believes that it was written after his return:

> We can also conclude that it [i.e., the encounter between Francis and the Sultan] resulted in the expansion of the Franciscan outlook. For Francis and his brothers added a chapter to their basic document which sanctioned the extension of their Christian service to men and women beyond the spheres of Christian life.[4]

Similarly, Jan Hoeberichts is very clear about when Chapter 16 was written:

> The precision with which Francis and the brothers formulated the two ways of presence among the Saracens favors Buhlmann's thesis. In other words, Francis' concrete experiences during his stay among the Saracens offer the best explanation for chapter 16, certainly for that part (1-9) which is explicitly concerned with the brothers who go among the Saracens. This holds true especially for the second way of presence in which Francis clearly indicated that the brothers could preach when they saw that it would please God. This can be interpreted as a general observation which is valid for

[3]Hoeberichts, *Francis and Islam* 45 and footnote 3 on pp. 216-17.
[4]David Flood, "Assisi's Rules and People's Needs," *Franciscan Digest* 2. 2 (1992): 69.

everyone, at all times and places: everyone must always and everywhere act in accordance with God's pleasure.[5]

Hoeberichts then goes on to say:

> The fact, however, that Francis used this expression precisely in this context, and thus seemed to relativize the necessity of preaching and baptizing for salvation, can only be explained, in my opinion, on the basis of a profound personal experience on Francis' part of the presence of God among the Saracens, a presence which Francis expressly wished to respect.[6]

Thus, I conclude that the *vision* of Francis, which impelled him to "go among the Saracens," had been defined as integral to his experience of Gospel life prior to his departure for the East – both in the lived experience of the brothers and in the *Early Rule*. I also believe that chapter 16 of the *Rule* was written after his experience at the Sultan's court. This could have been begun during the return trip, with editing and perhaps an insertion added in Italy.[7]

New insights gained from his travels expanded the horizon of Francis' vision. Hoeberichts agrees with Flood's argument that chapter 16 was inserted very purposefully after chapter 14 and before 17.[8] It connects with chapters 14 and 15 in terms of how the brothers are "to go throughout" the world. The fundamental attitude of humility (chapter 17), central to the brotherhood,

---

[5]Hoeberichts, *Francis and Islam* 46.

[6]Hoeberichts, *Francis and Islam* 46.

[7]Hoeberichts, *Francis and Islam* 47-49. Hoeberichts suggests that the verses about "obedience and the minister" may have been added after its' initial writing, after conflicts surfaced related to the mission to the Saracens. "Francis spoke with the Sultan. We do not know what transpired between them, save that the encounter came off humanly, to the honor of them both. Francis had not fallen victim to the propaganda of the Christian West. That, too, came from leaving the world. He journeyed to the Saracens as their brother and servant. That became movement policy, with Chapter 16 in the *Early Rule*, in a sharp rejection of the Church's policy toward the Saracens" 218, n 14.

[8]Flood ("Assisi's Rules" 70) states that Chapters 14 and 17 define the Franciscan mission in the world, with Chapter 16 explicitly including the Saracens in that mission.

was certainly a non-negotiable if the brothers are to carry their message to the Saracens. Indeed, it may be even more significant in light of encounters among non-Christians. With the placement of chapter 16 prior to 17, Francis is making it clear that the brothers must live humbly among the Saracens, offering them nothing less than the true peace of the Lord. This was to be proclaimed both in their greeting and the message they preach by their deeds.[9] The vision of Francis for this universal peace was intended for all people, everywhere. No one was to be excluded. All were included: the poor, lepers, outcasts, infidels. All were redeemed by the blood of Christ and all were meant to enjoy the fruits of Christ's love. This peace could only come about through loving and accepting the other, not by violence. Having experienced the violence of the Crusades first hand and having encountered a friend and a brother in "the enemy," Francis elaborated on how the brothers were to carry out their mission. Chapter 16 of the *Early Rule* is the result.

First Way of Being Present: Without Arguments or Disputes and in Submission

Francis' experience among the Saracens must have made the picture of God's vast design come into an even sharper focus. Knowing the typical attitude toward the Saracens, Francis uses the Scripture passage of sending the friars as "sheep among wolves" to introduce chapter 16. What Francis discovered in going to the Saracens, in humility and submission, was that these people were not ravenous wolves, but rather people with whom peace could be lived. "The lost paradise was restored, the eschatological vision of the kingdom of God, as described by Isaiah, was brought near: 'the wolf lives with the lamb' (11,6)."[10] The mission of these brothers among the Saracens was to end the hatred that existed by living among them and being subject to them. Thus would they "restore the original order of creation, the order of peace and harmony not only between human beings, but even between human beings and animals (cf. SalVirt

[9]Hoeberichts, *Francis and Islam* 49.
[10]Hoeberichts, *Francis and Islam* 63.

15-18)."[11] The striking thing is that this applies not only to the way of being among the Saracens, but applies to *all people* and *all situations* wherever the brothers are: they are always and everywhere to be peace-bearers by being humble and subject to all. They are choosing to live among the Saracens as peacemakers, not to fight them as crusaders. They believed and hoped that their submission and non-violent ways would be able to bring about the true peace for which they were willing to give their lives. This was the stance of Jesus and this was the only posture for the brothers minor. In striking contrast to the ecclesial and social "thesis of war and violence, Francis placed his antithesis of peace and nonviolence to which the Lord had inspired him when revealing to him the greeting: 'May the Lord give you peace' (*Testament* 23) a greeting whose meaning and implications he gradually discovered ever more."[12]

Chapter 16, verse 6 (*ER*) identifies the first of two ways of being present among the Saracens: "not to engage in arguments or disputes, but to be subject to every human creature for God's sake and to confess that they are Christians." This simple presence in submission is the very posture of Jesus, that of the loving obedience which is pleasing to God, and which must certainly produce fruit. Francis' requirement of submission is nothing less than a new approach to people and the whole of creation, thus a radical rejection of the existing structures of oppression. "It was an invitation to the brothers and to all people to build a new society, not on the foundations of violence and power which were inherent in the hierarchical structures of that time, but on the foundation of being subject to one another in love and tenderness which are signs of true brotherhood."[13] This act of "being subject" was by no means something passive. It was a free choice protesting the oppressive system of the day and witnessing to the true brother/sisterhood of God's reign restored in Jesus. After what Francis witnessed in the cruelty and

---

[11]Hoeberichts, *Francis and Islam* 64.
[12]Hoeberichts, *Francis and Islam* 69.
[13]Hoeberichts, *Francis and Islam* 77.

bloodshed of battle,[14] he was more convinced than ever that the only way to remove enmity between people was not to fight to subject others, but to be subject to them. This was not only a radical departure from the practice of the day, it was in direct opposition to canon law. "[S]everal decrees concerning the relations between Christians and Saracens, composed between 1188 and 1217, and later taken up in the *Decretales* of Gregory IX in 1234, presupposed or even stated explicitly that Christians may not be subject to Saracens."[15]

Part of "being subject" includes refraining from arguments and disputes. Such argumentation was very typical in scholastic and religious exchanges. Francis strictly forbids this. Hoeberichts suggests that arguments and disputes are counterproductive to handing on the truth. He then continues:

> [I]f truth is clothed with power, with a feeling of superiority, it is no longer itself and becomes unrecognizable for the other. It is no longer the gift freely offered to unite people with each other. It degenerates into a possession and hence into a means of power which leads to the condemnation and the exclusion of the other as a heretic. [. . .] Thus, Christianity wages war in the name of God who truly is love, and Christians feel themselves superior to others in the name of God who [. . .] is humility.[16]

---

[14]James of Vitry speaks about 60,000 casualties on Aug. 29, Oliver says it was only 30,000. When Damietta finally fell to the Crusaders, the atrocities done to the civilians were abominable.

[15]Hoeberichts, *Francis and Islam* 83.

[16]Hoeberichts, *Francis and Islam* 73. Hoeberichts examines sources (e.g., Celano Bonaventure, Ernoul) which depicts stories of Francis engaging in such argumentative exchange (pp. 73-74, 237-239). "It is evident that in the biographies little or nothing can be found of Francis' new approach, for the simple reason that it did not fit the ideas of the biographers, or rather their prejudices about Mohammed and Islam. This suggests that the stories about the disputes between Francis and the Saracens must be banished to the land of fables" (75).

For God's Sake

The basis for this approach was rooted in Francis' understanding of God. God was a God of humility, not of power as was the God of the Crusaders. The God of Jesus invited the brothers to imitate Jesus in inaugurating a new order of peace by subjecting themselves to all, even the Saracens. Thus, they engaged in this behavior, "for God's sake." And "because of this approach, the brothers were able to open themselves to everything they saw and heard among the Saracens, and thus create the space for new discoveries in a learning process that was full of surprises."[17] The results were astounding! For Francis found that God was here, alive in the Islamic history, traditions, rituals, prayers and even in the Saracens themselves! In their deep faith and reverent prayer, their respect for the Qur'an, their love of the names of God and their care for the poor, Francis discovered the very presence of God.

Second Way of Being Present:
To Proclaim the Word of God
When They See it Pleases the Lord

I will not belabor this point. However it must be mentioned, for it gives even greater emphasis to the preceding discussion on "being subject to." Surely it is proper and right for the brothers to proclaim God's word to the Saracens. However, there is a major condition applied to this activity. We have noted that *every* brother must unequivocally "not enter into disputes or arguments but be subject to." Now the *Early Rule* states that the second way to be present is "to proclaim the word of God *when* they see that it pleases the Lord" (italics mine). Thus, it could happen that the proclamation of the Word *never* happens, for it is contingent on it "pleasing the Lord." Hoeberichts calls attention to how James of Vitry's report of the exchange between Francis and the Sultan ended. As noted above, he asks Francis to "pray for him, that God would reveal to him the law and the faith which is more pleasing to Him." Might Francis have been

---

[17]Hoeberichts, *Francis and Islam* 89.

influenced by the Sultan's request and thus included in chapter 16 the same idea of "pleasing God?" Hoeberichts enlightens us:

> These words fit very well in the mouth of a Muslim. For one of the most important words which occurs over and over again in a conversation with a Muslim is *'in'shallah*, if it pleases Allah, if Allah wills it. Through the frequent use of this word, that very often serves as an interjection or exclamation, believing Muslims express their most profound conviction of faith, namely that their lives are completely in God's hands....everything in their lives centers around *islam*, around submission, surrender to the will of Allah.[18]

An astonishing insight is given to Francis. Because of his tremendous openness to God's lead (going back to having had his eyes opened as he had been led among the lepers), Francis knew he would meet God over and over in every place and in everyone. Thus, Hoeberichts tells us:

> Francis had come to greatly admire how it had pleased God to be actively present among them [Saracens] and to be the source of much good in their lives. He knew therefore that God had not rejected them, and had not left them to their own devices. On the contrary, even though they were different, God accepted them and was continually interested in them. And thus Francis too was ready to accept and to respect them for God's sake. Because of this positive approach, Francis was able to correct many wrong ideas about Islam and discover its many good qualities.[19]

Thus Francis finds his vision of universal fraternity enlarged and strengthened. Those to whom he went as brother-to-brother, were indeed, children of God. And somehow, in the "incomprehensible, unfathomable" mystery of God's goodness, "creator and savior of all" (*ER* 23:11), Francis penetrates ever deeper into God's majesty which transcends even Christianity and Christian theology. He is even able to let go of the question of the

---

[18]Hoeberichts, *Francis and Islam* 100.
[19]Hoeberichts, *Francis and Islam* 101.

Saracen's salvation, leaving that to God.[20] Francis realized that somehow, in the divine mystery, Islam too was part of God's pleasure and it too added to God's praise, glory and presence in the world.

Thus it is, that "when it pleases God," the brothers may proclaim God's Word. They are to do this in a way which establishes a unity between them: proclaiming faith in the all-powerful God, Creator of all, who alone is good. While proclaiming the Triune God, it is belief in ONE God, all-powerful, Creator, Good, which is a source of common ground between the faiths. Bap-

---

[20]Hoeberichts, *Francis and Islam* 101. Leonhard Lehmann examines this issue in his article "Francis's Two Letters to the Custodes: Proposals for Christian-Islamic Ecumenism in Praising God" *Greyfriars Review* 2:3 (1998): 63-91. He asks: "Does Francis of Assisi support the absolute claim of the Catholic Church that outside her there is no salvation [. . .] or does he – in the sense of an integrating universality of his faith in Jesus Christ – commit himself to more general religious aims with which both Christians and Muslims can agree?" (25). He concludes that Francis "probably agreed without much hesitation or questioning with the claim of the Church formulated by the IVth Lateran Council: outside the Church no salvation" (58). Nevertheless he goes on to say that while Francis promotes the claim of the absolute validity of the Catholic faith as is written in both the *Letter to the Rulers* and Chapter 16 of the *Earlier Rule*, he also leaves "a considerable space for the continued existence of other religions because of the new or rather the rediscovered evangelical method which prefers the example of life to preaching. [. . .] Hence the question: is it possible that Francis defends here the claim of the universal validity of the religious rather than of the catholic faith? In favour of a more universal, interconfessional intention is the fact that in his *Letters to the Custodians* and to the *Rulers* Francis explicitly assumes the Islamic *salat* into the Christian life of prayer. Does this not demonstrate an 'integrating universality' of his faith in Jesus Christ? Thus we may conclude that Francis, on the one hand, defends without any qualifications the absolute claim of the Church proclaimed by the Lateran Council and, on the other hand, presents, out of respect for believers of other religions, such general religious concerns that the obligatory character of the catholic faith is placed into a larger interconfessional context. Like in the *First Letter to the Custodians*, so also in the *Letter to the Rulers* Francis unites catholic firmness with a surprising ecumenical universality" (59-60). Lehmann also addresses this in his article "Francis's Two Letters to the Custodes: Proposals for Christian-Islamic Ecumenism in Praising God" *Greyfriars Review* 2:3 (1988) 63-91, particularly pages 80-81.

tism may come, yet that does not seem to be primary for Francis. What *is* primary is the *gospel witness*. Submission to God's pleasure is primary. Francis is clearly moving into new territory, yet this is what he hears the Spirit saying to him. Presence and "being subject to" are the radical form of proclamation that chapter 16 presents to the brothers who "go to" the Saracens. Constant listening to the Spirit of God, being directed by God, is mandatory. It must be God's agenda that is first, not the friar's, nor the Church's. Christian witness may lead to persecution, even martyrdom. If so, that too must be accepted. But that is in no way primary, even though it could be a consequence of their presence as brothers and as peacemakers. Living among the Saracens in the manner of Christ (humble, obedient, nonviolent, and peaceful), Francis saw the possibility of ending the enmity between Christians and Saracens and creating an atmosphere in which true peace could be established.[21]

Finally, it is in imitation of Jesus' love for his friends, for his "enemies," that this way of being among the Saracens is to be lived. Hoeberichts connects the ending of chapter 16 with Francis' understanding of love for one's enemy, especially as noted in Admonition 9, where Francis connects "love of one's enemies with love of God. [. . .] By injuring a neighbor, a brother or sister, the other person has violated the love of God for humankind and frustrated God's plan for a world in which all people live together as brothers and sisters."[22] However, by living as peacemakers with one another, we realize God's plan and work with God in bringing forth a deeper experience of God's reign. This is accomplished by embracing the Gospel life of Jesus and living his humble, obedient, nonviolent life of loving service.

Thus Francis articulates his new discovery about how the brothers are "to go through" the world, proclaiming the Good News of Jesus. The next event in Francis' life showed how seriously he listened to this truth.

---

[21]Hoeberichts, *Francis and Islam* 116.
[22]Hoeberichts, *Francis and Islam* 123-124.

The Resignation of Francis

At the Chapter of 1220, Francis resigned as "minister and servant" of the Order. Celano tells us that he did this "out of humility" and then attaches it to poor health.[23] His health was a legitimate factor in his resignation. He returned home from the Holy Land suffering from malaria, leprosy and trachoma. Problems in the Order (news of which had prompted that return) are well known.[24] Francis saw himself at odds with many in the Order and felt that the Order was slipping away from him. His life's project was changing and he must have been tempted to take control. Yet, he resigned. Were there reasons other than frustration and illness that contributed to his resignation?

The Assisi Compilation presents the power struggle occurring in the Order from which Francis chooses to step aside. Francis rejects "the power of this world" by handing the leadership of the Order over to others. He resigns in order to be "one who is lesser."

> When I renounced and gave up among the brothers, I excused myself before the brothers at the general chapter saying that, because of my illness I could not take care of them and care for them. And yet, if the brothers had walked and were still walking according to my will, for their consolation I would not want them to have any other minister except me until the day of my death.[...] My office, that is, a prelacy over the brothers, is spiritual, because I must overcome vices and correct them. Therefore, if I cannot overcome and correct them by preaching and example, I do not want to become an executioner who beats and scourges, like a power of this world. I trust in the Lord... until the day of my death, I

[23]*2C* 143.

[24]These problems included: 1) the tremendous expansion of the Order, both numerically and geographically; 2) increasing numbers of clerics who had a different understanding of the mission and lifestyle; 3) members who no longer had a connection to Francis or commitment to his original vision. A slightly different version is found in G.P. Freeman, H. Sevenhoven, "The Legacy of a Poor Man," *Franciscan Digest* 3.1 (1993): 1-19.

will not cease teaching the brothers by example and action to walk by the path which the Lord showed me, and which I showed and explained to them.[25]

Francis' deep commitment to his vision of how to live in this world influenced his resignation. Francis' constant prayer, from the earliest days of his conversion, was that he might know and do God's will. Francis was totally given to abandoning his own will and embracing the will of God. In his *Prayer before the Crucifix* Francis prayed "that I may carry out Your holy and true command." I suggest that his recent experience among the Saracens affirmed and deepened his commitment to "surrender to God's will" and affected his "letting go" of the Order. I believe Francis was deeply impressed by the centrality of submission (*islam*) in the lives of the Muslims. He certainly emphasized this in chapter 16 of the *Early Rule*. Now, possibly soon after having written that down, he heads to the Chapter. Aware of so many diverse opinions and directions among the brothers, Francis was forced to make a choice. Francis was a man who struggled with pride.[26] Given his captivating personality, he had to work at not letting his own will dominate. It was natural for Francis to want to control the project he had begun and had given his life to. His vision and the way to live out that vision was clear to Francis. At this time, he must have been tempted to get the Order "back on track," to have all the brothers united in a common expression of that vision. Yet Francis must also have asked himself: was this the time for *him* to submit and "be subject to" his own brothers? Could *this* be God's will for him – to simply "let go"? Was his last great gift to the Order to do what he asked of his brothers: to teach by example? In following the humility of Jesus, was he now being asked that he love his brothers by stepping down, by being "minor" and "subject to." Perhaps his encounter with *Islam* spoke to him now – that surren-

---

[25]*The Assisi Compilation* 106. Other "resignation" texts include *AC* 11; *LP* 76, 106 and 114; *2C* 158, 188, 151.

[26]*AC* 11 refers to this: "Blessed Francis wanted to be humble among his brothers. To preserve greater humility, [. . .] he resigned the office of prelate... [H]ere is Brother Peter di Catanio: let us all, you and I, obey him.".

der, even of one's life project, could be the precise sacrifice that was asked of him. Could there be a greater humility? A greater surrender? A deeper act of faith? Little did he know, there could be!

Letters (To the Clergy, Custodes, Rulers and The Entire Order)

After his resignation, Francis utilized letter writing as a way to offer guidance and direction to his followers. These writings continued to call people to a Gospel based vision of life. Francis' message was familiar – a call to penance and peacemaking through lives of obedience and humility. Obvious connections with the Muslim faith appear in these letters.[27] Whether as Jeusset asks, this is due to Islamic influence or simply a timely convergence of beliefs,[28] there are definite correlations. Scholars such as Gwénolé Jeusset and Francis De Beer suggest that the strong emphasis of the transcendence of God in Islam challenged Francis to rethink both the transcendence of God and God's immanence, resulting in an even stronger commitment to the otherness of God as well as to the awesomeness of the Incarnation. At the same time, it engendered a deeper acknowledgement of the Oneness of God.

A look at some of these connections are in order. In the *Letters to the Clergy* Francis exhorts all the clergy, not just members of his Order, to exercise the greatest care and reverence for the Body and Blood of the Lord as well as for "His most holy names and written words" (vv. 1,2,3,6). Francis asks the same of the custodes (*1LtCus* 2): to have "the greatest possible reverence for the Body and Blood of our Lord Jesus Christ, together with His holy name and the writings. . ." He continues by exhorting them, in every sermon to remind the people about penance and the Eucharist. They are also to preach the praise of God to "all nations, all people throughout the world at every hour and when-

---

[27]If we were able to compare more writings of Francis prior to his departure to the East with writings after his return, it would be easier to note influences from his trip. Since this is not possible, any conclusions about the influence of Islam cannot be claimed with certainty.

[28]Jeusset, *God is Courtesy* 52.

ever bells are rung" (v. 8). Leonhard Lehmann comments on the
request of Francis in this letter:

> Preaching penance, the reception of Holy Communion
> and Eucharistic devotion are closely connected with a
> song of praise to which the faithful are to be summoned
> by the ringing of a bell. Francis passes from one theme
> to the other with a simple "and" and evidently does not
> see preaching about public worship as "an entirely dis-
> tinct topic." [. . .] He wished the custodes to preach how,
> at the sound of the bell, praise and thanksgiving were
> to be shown to the Lord present in the Eucharist. There
> is no doubt that the text gives priority to devotion to the
> Eucharist, but it immediately moves on to the second
> theme: public worship. Since the text unites the two top-
> ics so closely, it is our belief that the "new signs" are not
> limited to the Eucharist. They include a public call to
> prayer.[29]

Lehmann goes on to suggest that this appeal of Francis was
influenced by the Muslim rite of *salat*[30] and that Francis may
have heard both the call of the muezzin as well and the *salat* as
"new signs" between heaven and earth.[31] Lehmann also points
out that the plural of the word for signs (*signa*) is used in the
Letter to the Custodes, thus indicating that the Eucharist, the
name and words of the Lord, the call to prayer and the public
prayer of praise are **all** "signs" connecting heaven and earth.
The phrase "heaven and earth" is of significance, as Francis uses

---

[29]Leonhard Lehmann, "Francis's Two Letters to the Custodes:
Proposals for Christian-Islamic Ecumenism in Praising God," *Greyfriars
Review* 2:3 (1998): 71.

[30]Lehmann ("Francis's Two Letters to the Custodes" 75-76) describes
salat as a combination of bodily postures and minutely ritualized prayer
consisting of 17 parts that must be meticulously carried out. During
this prayer the Muslim acknowledges Allah as the One and only God.
This prayer is offered five times each day and is announced by the
muezzin.

[31]Jeusset (*God Is Courtesy*, 45) agrees that Francis, like many others,
was "moved by the beauty of the call to prayer summoned by the
muezzin, and the grandeur of the prostration of Muslims in the dust of
the camp at Damietta."

it frequently in articulating his universal vision.[32] As previously stated this phrase is often used in Islamic writings. The vision of universal unity/fraternity has now grown to include even specific practices from Islam. The scope of his vision is proclaimed as we note those to whom this message ought to be announced: *all* nations, such that praise and thanks might be given to God by *all people throughout the world*[33] at every hour and whenever bells are rung (italics mine). Lehmann states:

> Francis envisages a practice meant to endure for all times and to be disseminated among all people. [. . .] The custodes are not to limit their preaching of the divine praises to the people of their immediate surroundings but to carry it to the peoples of the entire world. Francis entrusts his custodes and preachers with a universal mission transcending all national boundaries.[34]

Thus, we see again that Francis' vision of universal fraternity has been impacted by his visit among the Muslims both in his personal experience of brotherhood with the Sultan and a discovery of religious practices which could serve to unite peoples who were thought to have nothing in common, and more importantly, had every reason to hate each other. So convinced that peace and mutual respect was possible between the two faiths, Francis worked at achieving this from multiple approaches. A new way of thinking was demanded. New behaviors were demanded. Nothing less than a revolution was needed. Thus, not only did he ask his custodes and all the clergy to get involved in this, he also addresses the rulers of the peoples, Christian and non-Christian. Francis calls the rulers themselves to conversion and asks that they take seriously their responsibility to call their people to the same. In *The Letter to the Rulers* Francis speaks of a herald who would call the people to prayer. This is similar to the bells that would do the same, proposed in *The First Letter to the Custodes*. As Lehmann states:

---

[32]*Lt Ord* 12-13, *OfP* ps 7:4; ps 14:6; ps 15:9, *Praises Before All the Hours* 7-8, as noted by Lehmann, "Francis's Two Letters to the Custodes" 72.

[33]*ab universo populo per totam terram.*

[34]Lehmann, "Francis's Two Letters to the Custodes" 75.

Both letters have the same goal in mind. They are addressed to important "multiplicators." The superiors and preachers of the order are to explain the sign and its purpose to all the people. The rulers of the city-states ought to adopt the Muslim custom and incorporate it in their statutes. The ultimate goal is the praise of God rising up from "all the peoples of the earth." Francis felt compelled to proclaim this idea of a joint Muslim and Christian praise of God loud and clear, because such an ecumenical witness, a sign of uniting two hostile religions in prayer, was unheard of and even unthinkable for people accustomed to preaching of crusades and whose minds were filled with hatred of Islam.[35]

Francis' unbounded enthusiasm for praying "at every hour" by all the people (*1Lt Cus* 8) is made more reasonable in the *Letter to the Rulers* where he asks that "every evening an announcement be made by a messenger or some other sign" (v. 7). This harkens back to the Islamic muezzin. Lehmann concludes that it was the time Francis spent among the Saracens that gave him this idea of the public call to prayer.

The worldwide scope of his plan can be understood against his experiences there. It was there that Francis saw the Muslims, at the call of the muezzin, kneel down, bow toward Mecca and pray to Allah the Almighty. The sight made such a deep impression on him that he himself would often add gestures to his prayers. In a world bent on conquest, he felt in the cry of the muezzin and the prayer-response of the faithful an omen of something that might unite the two warring factions of the human race.[36]

Building on his belief in the One God of all peoples, even non-Christian, Francis was able to appreciate the religious tradition of the Muslims. His spirit of tolerance and acceptance was not rooted in a spirit of religious syncretism but rather in the deepest respect which each son/daughter of God deserves. Francis' vision of universal fraternity, strongly confirmed by his

[35]Lehmann, "Francis's Two Letters to the Custodes" 76.
[36]Lehmann, "Francis' Two Letters to the Custodes" 77.

experience among the Saracens, brought him to desire and work for building a bridge between the Muslims and Christians. His commitment to living a life of penance and praise of God could be assisted by a practice such as *salat*. Thus, Francis' vision saw all people everywhere, in different languages and even different faiths, united in praise of this One God, Creator of all. He asked the help of his custodes, of the Rulers of the people and the entire order in achieving this. Francis deBeer also identifies an influence from Islam in *The Letter to the Entire Order*. "When you hear His *name*, the *name* of that Son of the Most High, our Lord Jesus Christ, [. . .] *adore His name with fear and reverence, prostrate on the ground!*" (v. 4, italics mine). The letter goes on to speak to the brothers who are sent into the world to bring everyone to know that He alone is Almighty. Striking are the connections between the prostrations of the Muslims and the reverence for the name of God who is One and Almighty. Then this letter goes on to speak of the profound mystery of the Body and Blood of Christ, the gift of God incarnate. For Francis, the "sublime humility" as well as the "humble sublimity" of God (v 27) verbalizes the paradox of God's imminence and transcendence.[37] Francis articulates this truth with even greater clarity and passion having listened to the voices of Islam in the court of al-Kamil. "There is no conclusive proof that Francis's ordinance is to be derived from the Islamic *Salat*, but a direct connection here is very probable."[38]

Francis' Experience on Mt. La Verna[39]

After the defeat of the crusaders in Egypt at the Battle of Baramun, August 29, 1221, Damietta was surrendered to the

[37]F. De Beer (p. 107) states: "the Incarnation, henceforth, became for Francis the sign of 'sublime humility and humble sublimity.'"

[38]Anton Rotzetter, "Francis of Assisi: A Bridge to Islam," *Frontier Violations: The Beginnings of New Identities*, ed. Felix Wilfred and Oscar Beozzo *Concilium 1999/2* (Maryknoll: Orbis, 1999) 111.

[39]Primary sources for this experience include: *1C* 91-96, *2C* 135-138, *LMj* 13:1-9 (especially 1-3). This section also relies on the unpublished work of Michael Cusato, both from class lectures (Fall of 2001) and private discussions.

Sultan al-Kamil and the crusaders left Egypt. This failure was unacceptable to both Pelagius and Honorious III. Thus, by April 1222, plans for another military campaign were being formulated[40] — this time in concert with Frederick II whose betrothal to the daughter of John of Brienne would make him King of Jerusalem. After a series of delays, a new, major attack on the Holy Land was therefore planned for April 1225. Plans for this were announced in July 1224.

In August 1224, Francis, accompanied by Brother Leo, Illuminato, Angelo, Rufino, Masseo and other companions, traveled to Mt. La Verna to spend the Lent of St. Michael (August 15-September 29). It is very likely that Francis went to La Verna profoundly depressed or deeply discouraged by the news of the new campaign. Francis had left Egypt five years before. During these years, he had been preaching penance and peacemaking – both by word and example –and sharing the vision of the brotherhood/sisterhood of all God's creatures. Francis yearned that the human fraternity, saved by the passion of Christ, not be further destroyed by bloodshed. Francis surely continued to pray for his friend, Sultan Malek al-Kamil, and perhaps even held out hope that al-Kamil would continue to desire the peace that Christ desired for all (and which al-Kamil had attempted to effect in his five peace offers between 1219-1221 during the Damietta siege). Perhaps Francis hoped that God would use al-Kamil to bring about this peace, bringing forth "fruits worthy of penance" represented by the mystery of the Tau.[41] Would not

[40]Powell, *Anatomy of a Crusade* 196.

[41]The *tau* (the Greek letter "T") is rich in symbolic meaning, particularly when it comes to be associated in Christian history with the theology of the cross and repentance. The tau is originally identified in the passage from Ezekiel 9 as a "saving sign." The man wrapped in linen marks the tau on the foreheads of the men who sigh and weep over Jerusalem. It is a sign connected to the saving act of God in the Passover event. In the decree of the Fourth Lateran Council, *Quia maior*, the tau – thanks to its association with the victory of Christ on the cross in Jerusalem – came to be used as the pre-eminent sign for the crusaders who were taking up the banner of Christ and risking even death by fighting against the enemies of Christ, the Saracens. Francis' understanding of the tau would stand in marked contrast to the meaning given to it by this Council, a sign which, in effect, justified

this also be a *jihad* in its truest, deepest sense (*The Greater Jihad*)? Would this not be a true surrender to God's will? And would not this be what both religions found at their very core: the peace, harmony, right relationship that is God and is God's will? We have seen that al-Kamil shared a desire for peace with Francis. Even though Francis knew there were differences separating him from the Sultan and other Saracens, he also knew there was an undeniable connection: he was their brother and they were brothers and sisters to him. This was true because of the universal fraternity established in Christ who was brother to all and whose blood had been shed for the redemption of all. He also knew that they shared common values. As Francis went to La Verna to pray, the request of the Sultan must have been strong in his heart: "Pray that God might reveal to me the path which is most pleasing to Him."

At La Verna, Francis separated himself from the others, building a hut out of branches, as did the others. Leo served him bread and water during his fast. According to the sources during the Lent of St. Michael in 1224, Francis was filled with longing to know God's will.[42] He spends his days in prayer, deep in communion with God. At one point we are told, he *threw himself on the ground* and begged for light in the darkness of his heart. Then, he consulted the Scriptures. He is directed to pray over the Passion of Jesus. On the feast of the Holy Cross (September 14) he prays for two graces: to feel in his body and soul the *pain* Christ felt in his passion and the *love* Christ felt to suffer for human beings. Then he experienced the vision of the

and gave religious meaning to the crusades. For Francis the tau also represented the saving event of Christ's sacrifce on the cross but as expressed specifically in a way of life that he calls "doing penance." As we have already seen, to "do penance," for Francis, meant living a life that affirmed (not derogated) all members of the human community; reconciled (not divided) the human family; worked to understand as brother and sister (not destroy as an enemy) creatures, like himself, created by the same God. Indeed, so important was this sign for Francis that he frequently signed his letters and marked beams and windowsills in prayer places and cells of the friars with the same tau. The *tau* will also be prominently displayed on the *chartula* which will be more fully examined later in this chapter.

[42]*1C* 91-96; *AC* 118; *LMj* 13:2-3; *LP* 93.

Seraph. After the vision, marks of the five wounds of Christ appear on his body. In thanksgiving for this great grace, Francis writes his prayer: *The Praises of God*. The parchment that this is written on is extant, a precious treasure kept today in the Sacro Convento in Assisi. A second writing of Francis appears on the back side of this *chartula*: *The Blessing to Brother Leo*; this side of the *chartula* also contains a large Tau cross and an enigmatic drawing near the bottom of the document. Finally this side of the *chartula* contains words written by Leo explaining the circumstances under which the writing occurred. I believe this event on Mt. La Verna and the writings which are part of it also have a connection to Francis' experience among the Saracens and his encounter with the Sultan.

Praises of God[43]

The importance of the Muslim prayer "The Ninety-Nine Beautiful Names of God" has already been noted, as has been the tremendous respect the Muslims have for the Name of God and the Holy Qur'an. During his stay in Damietta, Francis was surely impressed by the Muslims who fingered their prayer beads, praising God by repeating the divine attributes and names. Did Francis, bursting with praise for God after his mystical encounter with the Seraph, find himself addressing his God who was so "indescribable, ineffable, incomprehensible, unfathomable" (*ER* 23: 11) as the Muslims had done?[44] Jeusset suggests that Francis was influenced by his exposure to the Names of God prayed by the Saracens, adapting it, of course, to a Christian reality.

---

[43]The text of the *Praises of God* is found in Appendix 2, page 83.

[44]See Jeusset, *God is Courtesy* 45-53. The Qur'an reads: "Say: Invoke God or invoke the most merciful God. Whatever be the name under which you call upon him, the most beautiful name belongs to him (17:110). Jeusset calls attention to *ER* 23: 5 : "we are not worthy to call upon your name" which, before and after gives more than 40 names for God, which in vv. 9 and 11 speak in the indirect manner found in Islam: "... our Creator [...] who is the most complete [...] who is unspeakable, ineffable [...] etc. 46.

It is possible that the cult for the names of God discovered in the Orient had influenced the Poverello to mul-
tiply them in his prayer, but in a Trinitarian, Christic
and Eucharistic context. [. . .] Jesus is for Francis the
source of our knowledge of the names of God. But he
goes still farther, Jesus is the Name even of God: On
hearing his name, adore him with fear and reverence,
prostrating to the ground; his name is: Lord Jesus Christ,
Son of the Most High (LtOrd 4).[45]

Obviously, the strict monotheism of Islam is shared by Christianity. Yet the Christian Trinity presents a problem for Muslims. For one who wanted to find some common ground, or who
simply "saw" real connections, it was possible to acknowledge a
truth of each religion: both professed that God is One. Jeusset
quotes an unpublished study by Paul-Marie Demarquet which
points out that after Damietta, Francis "insists on the one God
side by side with the Trinity."[46] Evidence of this is found in the
Praises of God: "You are three and one" (3); *Letter to the Entire
Order:* "In the name of the Most High Trinity and holy unity"
(1); "You who live and rule in perfect Trinity and simple Unity"
(52); *Early Rule:* "Lord God Almighty in Trinity and in Unity"
(21:2), "Supreme Eternal God, Trinity and Unity (23:11), and "
God, Who is All-powerful, Three and One" (24:2). Indeed these
last verses of the *Early Rule* were probably written after his
return from the East. Zweerman and Goorbergh tell us: "Unlike
other prayers by Francis, the *Praises of God* do not conclude
with a Trinitarian doxology. However, this prayer relates en-
tirely to the mystery of the Triune God."[47] Related to this, I find

---

[45]Jeusset, *God is Courtesy* 49. Anton Rotzetter agrees with this, noting
it is particularly striking how Francis stands out in regards to an
unusual reverence for the name and word Jesus, even giving it pre-
eminence over the sacrament: "it is the word which makes the sacrament
the sacrament. . ." Rotzetter, "Francis of Assisi: A Bridge to Islam" 110.
It is interesting to note that there are 33 beads used for praying the
"Ninety-Nine Beautiful Names of God" and 33 invocations to God in
the *Praises of God.*

[46]Jeusset, *God is Courtesy* 48.

[47]Goorbergh and Zweerman, *Respectfully Yours, Signed and Sealed,
Francis of Assisi* (St. Bonaventure: Franciscan Institute, 2001) 254.

it interesting that "The Father" is the only one of the three divine Persons mentioned by name. Might this lack of a Trinitarian doxology and addressing God by only "Father" have any connection to Francis' experience among the Saracens? Might we be seeing a sensitivity to Islam in this expression of praise?[48]

In the *Praises of God* both the transcendence and immanence of God are acknowledged: God is Exalted and Near, and God is One and Triune. Jeusset cites other references to Francis' devotion to the name of Jesus (*LtOrd* 34-35, *Test* 10, 12) and wonders whether, having been exposed to the veneration of the Qur'an and the Names of God, Francis might have had a "rediscovery of the Word of God" and a "renewal, but by contrast with Muslim belief, of the faith in the Word Incarnate in the womb of the Virgin Mary and in the Eucharist."[49] Could all this that had been alive in Francis for the past five years have now been expressed in his beautiful, graced prayer *The Praises of God*? (Correlations between the Muslim prayer on the "Names of God" and Francis' *Praises of God* are contained in Appendix 1.)

The *Blessing to Brother Leo* and the Picture[50]

On the reverse side of the *Praises of God* Francis wrote out the blessing from the Book of Numbers (6:24-26). Further below he also drew a picture: the image of a large Tau cross emerging either out of the mouth of a head or from behind the head. The head is then circumscribed by some kind of border. Years later, Brother Leo added some words explaining how this *chartula* came to be. Traditional interpretations about the draw-

---

[48]Goorbergh and Zweerman (*Respectfully Yours* 247) point out that the word "our" is used in the prayer seven times. "Surely this 'our' indicates Francis' awareness of praying in union with the Church." In light of our considerations regarding Islam, might Francis (by his use of 'our') also be including even those who are *not* Christian? Might he be including the Saracens in his prayer, the people whose prayer he was so touched by, and through whom he came to an even greater understanding of God?

[49]Jeusset, *God is Courtesy* 53.

[50]The following development is based on the recent, yet unpublished, research of Michael Cusato.

ing identify either a skull or head assigned to either Adam or Leo. The most accepted theory is that it is a head (not a skull) of Leo who is placed under the protection of the Tau. Based on the work of De Beer, Fleming and most recently Cusato, I would like to suggest another possibility. Namely, that it would not be impossible to conceive that the *chartula* was intended for the Sultan, and has a message for us about Francis' ongoing conversion to the vision and plan of God regarding the universal fraternity of God's creation.

The blessing consists of two parts: the words consisting of 5 lines above and, under the arms of the Tau, two additional lines of unequal length and the picture, which present a united message.[51] The words are virtually verbatim from Numbers 6:24-26 except that the word "Lord" is mentioned only once. By the unique placement of the words in the last sentence, with the Tau in the midst of them, Fleming suggests that Francis has constructed a cryptogram, a hidden message. The Tau is surely the dominant feature of this section and Fleming suggests that Francis began with the Tau and fit the letters around it. If, therefore, the Tau is used as the letter "t" for the message, then the line

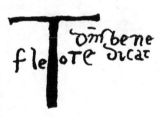

which has been translated as : "The Lord bless, Brother Leo, (*f leo*) you" becomes "Well may the Lord say, You shall weep" or possibly "Let the Lord say, "Well shall you weep." The key word for Fleming (as well as for Cusato) is thus *fletote*. Is the message written "*f leo te*" or *fletote*? We are reminded of the references to weeping found in the Muslim tradition, particularly among the Sufis. Bonaventure (*LMj*, Prologue: 2) also links Francis' role as the writer of the Tau with the penitential mission of calling people to weep.[52] Bonaventure has taken this text

[51]The information related to the blessing of Leo is taken from John Fleming, "The Iconographic Unity of the Blessing for Brother Leo," *Franziskanische Studien* 63 (1981) 203-220.

[52][. . .] not only does this advance the mission he held of calling to weep and mourn, to shave one's head and wear sackcloth and to sign the Tau on the foreheads of those moaning and grieving with a sign of a penitential cross... Fleming 209.

from Isaiah 22:12 where it is the *Lord* who calls for weeping. Again, Fleming believes that this is the scriptural text Francis had it mind. Using Isaiah and the blessing from *Numbers* would be very easy and typical of Francis. We know of Francis' devotion to the Trinity. In the classical tradition this blessing was viewed as one of the Old Testament witnesses to the Trinity because of its three phrases introduced by the word "Lord." In addition, the Tau itself was also a "sign" of the Trinity. Equally important is the context of this blessing: an episode from the Exodus, the central Old Testament event which establishes the covenant between God and God's people. Here God orders Moses to order Aaron and his sons to bless the children of Israel. The

From Ms 344 of Biblioteca Comunale in Assisi (14th century)

larger context concerns the Nazarites, the main ascetic order in ancient Judaism, seen as precursors of Christian monks. Could Francis also have seen the Sufis included in this story, ever ancient, ever new?[53]

Francis drew a head. Easily identified is the chin with the suggestions of whiskers or a beard. The profile of the head also indicates the forehead, nose and mouth. The top of the head is drawn with very definite lines, to which we will return. The

[53]Fleming 210-211.

large Tau cross rises from behind the lower jaw or possibly from the mouth itself. Fleming (relying on the analysis of Oktavian von Rieden) gives two reasons why this is *not* the head of Leo: 1) the Tau is not marked on the forehead and 2) the "most prominent feature" of the drawing, (the jagged outline surrounding the head) must be the "grave of Adam." Fleming disagrees with von Rieden only in identifying the most prominent feature of the drawing: for Fleming, it must be the Tau, binding together the words and picture to offer the blessing. As a letter, the Tau is the key to the cryptogram *fletote*; as a picture it is the key which unlocks the unity of the *chartula*![54] I agree with them that the head is not Leo's. I also agree with Fleming that the Tau is key to unlocking the mystery of the *chartula*. However, in addition to unlocking the mystery of the message, I believe it might also unlock the mystery of the original recipient. I believe the head could be the clue to the original recipient of the *chartula*, and that, if this is true, it is neither the head of Leo nor of Adam. Before considering that any further, we must look briefly at the meaning of the Tau for Francis.

The Tau has important connections with the history of the Exodus and Fleming believes that Francis is making reference to that in the *chartula*. Francis is also drawing on the man dressed in linen from Ezekiel (Chapter 9) and the angel of the sixth seal from Revelations (7:2) who signs the servants of God on their foreheads. The Hebrew *taw*, the final letter of the alphabet, actually means "sign" or "mark." The two most important of these "saving signs" were connected with the Exodus: 1) the blood-mark of the Passover; and 2) the fiery serpent (Numbers 21). The people grumbled against God who sent the fiery serpents. The people died after the serpents bit them. The people repented, Moses intervened and God relented. "Make a fiery serpent and set it on a pole . . . those who looked upon it, lived (Numbers 21: 6-9). Jesus refers to this: "As Moses lifted up the serpent in the wilderness, even so must the Son of Man be lifted up" (John 3:14). Both the blood-daubed door-posts and the pole of the brazen serpents were visualized as Taus, as of course was the cross of Christ. It seems that Francis "deliberately collated

[54]Fleming 215.

the words of Aaron with the mark of Aaron to speak of penance and salvation in the Age of Grace."[55]

In Ezekiel 6 the man dressed in linen marks a Tau on the foreheads of the men that sigh and that weep for all the abominations of Jerusalem, that is, of a penitent and righteous remnant; likewise, in Revelations 7, it is the "servants of God" marked with the tau by the angel of the 6th seal. Bonaventure associates Francis with the mission of Isaiah 22:12: "to summon all men to mourn and lament, to shave their heads and wear sackcloth." Says Fleming: "The Tau is a redemptive sign, but only for those prepared to flee Egypt in the dead of night with small baggage, to repent of glutching against God, to weep for the sins of the City of Man."[56]

Remembering that Francis' profound experience of communion with God occurred in the context of the Feast of the Holy Cross, it is noteworthy to observe that the protective power of the cross is one of the themes of this feast. The Offertory prayer of the feast prays: "Through the sign of the holy cross, Lord *protect your people* against every snare of all *enemies* (italics mine)."[57] This is also prayed in the Eucharistic Prayer.

Having gone to La Verna to spend 40 days in prayer, and having been directed by God to pray with the Passion of the Lord, with the request of the Sultan that Francis would pray for him, with the deep longing in his heart of the peace of God to be known to all humankind and all of creation, Francis was faced with the mystery of redemption in the Exodus story which is fulfilled in Jesus. Like Jesus, Francis knew no enemy, only brothers. Like Jesus, Francis longed for unity, "that all might be one." Nowhere was that unity more needed than between Christians and Muslims. And so, having never given up hope for peace with his Muslim brothers and sisters, he prays for the Saracens on La Verna. Might Francis have prayed that the Sultan would be given the grace to accept Christ and to embrace a life of penance and peace in Christ's Most Holy Name? Might Francis have seen peace coming to the Holy Land through the goodness of

---

[55]Fleming 219.

[56]Fleming 219.

[57]Zweerman and Goorbergh 245.

God manifested in the works of the Sultan? Surely he longed and prayed for this. He writes a blessing of God (the God of Mohammad and Jesus) for his friend, the Sultan, using a Trinitarian formula, yet *adapting* it out of respect for his brother who worships the God who is One. He prays:

> May God bless you and keep you,
> Show you His face and be merciful to you,
> Turn His face toward you and give you peace.

Perhaps Francis, deep in prayer and union with God, enflamed by the same love of Christ, the very love of Christ's passion, even now burning in his body, as it had long burned in his heart, prayed the blessing for the Sultan – a blessing from a Triune yet One God – and literally "drew" the picture of its fulfillment: peace (represented by the Tau) coming to the Holy Land. Then, confirmed anew in this vision of universal fraternity, the praises of God, "our" God – the God of the Muslims and the Christians and all people everywhere – burst forth from the heart of Francis and onto the parchment. For this is what gives true praise to God: THIS vision that is right out of the heart of God. THIS world in which the barriers separating people were removed; THIS dream of universal fraternity and peace; THIS love which removes all barriers, allows one to call the "enemy" friend, and opens one's eyes and heart to see that "enemy" as brother/sister.

Truly the *Praises of God* reflect the Mystery of the Cross, now living even more profoundly in the person/body of Francis. Truly this All-Good God has once again led Francis "to do penance" by taking him among his brothers and sisters; not the lepers this time (who were the outcasts and invisible members of society), but the enemy (evil itself.) Yes, God indeed does wondrous things! He opens the eyes and heart of Francis to embrace in an even more profound way the truth of universal fraternity.

Fleming says that there is a deep mystery in this blessing which is thrilling in its revelation of historical and theological consciousness. How much I agree. He assigns this blessing to Leo. I assign it to Malek al-Kamil but use Fleming's words:

> Francis had a double message: as assurance of the power
> of God's protective grace, but also a call to penance. He
> blessed him with the words with which Aaron had

blessed the children of the Exodus, for he was one of
those whom Francis characteristically thought of as the
Exodus of the new age, [. . .] He blessed him with that
special sign by which God had in ancient times prefig-
ured the definitive symbol of salvation. [. . .] But he at
once called him to mourning and lamentation, [. . .] for
those on whom the tau is marked must sigh and weep
for the abominations of Jerusalem. *Dominus bene
"fletote" dicat.*[58]

Francis De Beer believes that the real recipient was the Sultan himself AND that the head is also that of the Sultan. "In
our opinion, it is the head of a Saracen, and more precisely that
of the sultan. Compare Francis's graphic with the sultan in
Giotto's fresco at the Basilica of Assisi. The analogy is a striking
one."[59] Note the similarities between the headdresses and beards.
In studying the picture Francis drew, De Beer says: "the intensity of the Sultan staring at the Tau is overwhelming." He thus

[58]Fleming 220.
[59]De Beer, *We Saw Brother Francis* 109.

concludes that the Tau is coming out of the mouth of the Sultan, showing the Sultan confessing the cross. De Beer also suggests that the outline represents the Holy Land, inside of which is the Sultan professing the Tau. "It would be the most extraordinary judgment passed on the Crusade by Francis himself, that the Holy Places no longer belonged any more to the Christians than to Islam."[60] In light of the evidence of De Beer and the work of Cusato, I suggest that the Tau is meant to be used as the letter "t" to formulate the phrase "Well may the Lord say, 'You shall weep'" or possibly, "Let the Lord say, 'Well shall you weep.'" Thus, the "Blessing" could well have been intended for the Sultan, the one Francis continued to pray for, especially in the context of his prayer during those forty days: The Passion of Our Lord Jesus Christ.

The *Canticle of the Creatures*[61]

The very vision that Francis had been graced with – first as he was led among the lepers, then deepened among the Saracens, and finally confirmed on Mt. La Verna in the stigmata – was about to be brought to fullness. The time is now the winter of 1224 and Francis' body is racked with pain. Perhaps the suffering in his soul was even more severe. Eloi Leclerc tells us:

> The evangelical values of pure simplicity, poverty and peace that were, in his eyes, so essential to the revelation of divine Love, had been shunted aside in a Christendom engrossed by power and ruled by the idea of the crusades. They were even questioned at times by his own followers. It was eventide in Francis' life, but he still had not experienced the full peace that evening should bring.[62]

---

[60]De Beer, "St. Francis and Islam," *Francis of Assisi Today,* ed. Christian Duquoc and Casiano Floristan, *Concilium 149* (New York: Seabury, 1981): 20.

[61]Sources: *2C* 213, 214; *AC* 83, 84; *LP* 43. The text of the *Canticle* is found in Appendix 2, page 143.

[62]Eloi Leclerc, *The Canticle of Creatures: Symbols of Union,* trans. Matthew O'Connell (Chicago: Franciscan Herald Press, 1977) ix.

The sources tell us that Francis, in constant pain, goes to San Damiano. For more than 50 days he was unable to bear the light of the sun during the day or fire at night. The pain was so great he could not sleep. Mice ran over him, distracting his prayer. One night, pitying himself, he asked God's help to bear this affliction with patience. He was told: "Brother, [. . .] be glad and rejoice in your illnesses and troubles, because as of now, you are as secure as if you were already in my kingdom."[63] He knew now for certain that he was suffering with Christ. He called his companions together in the morning and shared his joy with them:

> I must rejoice greatly in my illnesses and troubles and be consoled in the Lord, giving thanks always to God the Father, to His only Son, our Lord Jesus Christ, and to the Holy Spirit for such a great grace and blessing. In His mercy he has given me, His unworthy little servant living in the flesh, the promise of His kingdom. Therefore for His praise, for our consolation and for the edification of our neighbor, I want to write a new Praise of the Lord for his creatures. . .[64]

The result is his famous *Canticle of the Creatures*. It is not possible to understand the *Canticle* without understanding the suffering Francis was experiencing. His daily struggle to embrace the way of Christ in this suffering was consistent with his lifelong pursuit of walking with Christ. The *Canticle* is the ultimate expression of his vision of fraternal life, the life of brotherhood and sisterhood, rooted in Christ. That fraternal relationship which is true peace, asks each member and species of creation only what was asked of Christ: total obedience to God, that is, humble submission to the will of God. This 'yes' to being what one was created to be, *and nothing more*, is the essence of

---

[63]*AC* 83.

[64]*AC* 83. The Canticle was composed in 3 stages: vv. 1-9 (and possibly 14) at San Damiano, winter 1224-1225; vv. 10-11, June-Aug. 1225 during the civil war between the mayor and bishop; vv. 12-13 in 1226, when he was very near death.

peaceful harmony. In that God is truly praised. Thus, the vision
of Francis finds its fulfillment as he prays:

> Most High, all-powerful, good Lord,
> Yours are the praises, the glory, and the honor,
> and all blessing,
> To You alone, Most High do they belong,
> And no human is worthy to mention Your name. . .

Leclerc speaks of the upward movement of the first four stanzas, oriented to the transcendent God who is Most High. "Most
High," used three times in the first four stanzas, expresses
Francis' desire for God. Francis also identifies a posture of humility and poverty before God ("no one is worthy to mention
[God's] name"). Having established this upward movement toward the transcendent God, Francis shifts to a horizontal movement. He turns to creatures – that visible universe which will
be the path of praise to the Sacred. The one who acknowledged
that he was unworthy to mention God's name, now identifies
himself as brother to all creatures. This is the same movement
Francis experienced when he was led among the lepers – he
found himself in relation to others. He found in the lepers brothers and sisters, and the presence of God. He found the same
among the Saracens. Now he finds in all of creation – both in
the heavens and on earth – the presence of God, he finds brothers and sisters. All creatures form one large family in Christ,
whose death and resurrection is at the center of the history which
unites all that has been separated.

What stands out so strongly in this text is the sense of creation as *reconciled space*. Creation is that place where everything is in harmony, *where everything is in relation as brother /
sister*. This is portrayed in the first nine verses where humans
do not appear. In these verses everything is "being itself," in its
proper place, carrying out its function. Thus, there is a celebra-
tion of order and harmony as all exists in relationship. Humans
do not appear here because they do not enjoy this harmony. They
are at odds with each other. When they do appear, it is in the
context of *pardon* and *reconciliation*! They do belong in this creation when they too, like the other creatures, carry out *their*

function – when they are what they are and nothing else. And that is precisely, to "pardon and to bear their sufferings." This is what it means to be human: to be weak, limited and vulnerable. The only way humans can become part of the song of creation is to do what Jesus did in the Incarnation: to accept the human condition in all its limitations: to pardon and forgive and accept the suffering that is part of the human condition. When that happens, then humans can take their place in the song of praise to God.[65] When that happens, we find that the term "Most High," which was dropped after the fourth stanza, reappears. However, it no longer expresses a distant and inaccessible transcendent One. This transcendent One is now present to the person who desires mercy and peace. It is the path of reconciliation that takes one to the Most High. This Most High God then sets a crown on the one who acts in such a way![66]

So it is that the *Canticle* celebrates the human integration as a part of the family of the cosmos that is meant to be the home of all the brothers and sisters. This takes the understanding of universal fraternity much further than it had ever been taken. It comes from Francis' experience of Christ and what it means to be brother and sister, what it means to live in the world. The basic attitude of Francis – "to You alone most High do they belong and no one is worthy to mention your name" – explains it all. That radical understanding of poverty is the basis of the acceptance of Francis' humanness. The final integration of his vision has occurred. Being humble and submissive is at the core of it. Simply letting things be what they are to be is the key to enduring in peace. "Blessed are they who endure in peace, for by You, most High, they will be crowned." Francis now understands the depth of the message of repentance, poverty and peace. Everything must be as it was intended to be for peace to reign. For the human person that includes being obedient and "subject to." In a revolutionary text, Francis even speaks of human beings as "subject to" mother earth ("who sustains and governs us"), for God has established creation in such a way that

[65]These ideas are taken from the class lecture of Michael Blastic, February 21, 2002.
[66]Leclerc 33-34.

the earth governs humankind.[67] Leclerc says "From beginning to end, it [The Canticle] is a serene assertion of universal brotherhood. [. . .] The very names "Brother" and "Sister" given to sub-human things show a quite different manner of presence to the world than that which is characterized by the will to dominate and possess things."[68] No, humans are not in charge, God is!

And so humanity joins in the cosmic praise and is "brother" or "sister" by pardoning and bearing infirmity. The penultimate experience for the human person is to accept Sister Bodily Death, for through her God's will is accomplished and life begins anew.[69] For all this, people are to praise and bless the Lord and give Him thanks, and serve Him with great humility. We note that the last word of the Canticle is, literally, "humility." We know that for Francis it is also the first word.

The genius of Francis comes through in the two movements contained in the Canticle: the upward movement toward the transcendent God and the vertical movement toward communion with all of creation. "It is by no means to be taken for granted that these two should meet and join. In fact, their union is quite exceptional. [. . .] The surprising thing is that two such opposite movements should here be in perfect harmony."[70] Leclerc speaks

---

[67]Francis' *Salutation of the Virtures* also comes to mind, in which obedience makes us subject to all, even to the wild animals. For Francis, obedience always brings about relationship. THAT is the core of his vision of universal fraternity. It stems from the relationality which is at the heart of the mystery of God, Three in One.

[68]Leclerc 3, 10. (This notion certainly challenged the traditional Jewish-Christian understanding of subdue and govern.)

[69]Goorbergh and Zweerman (*Respectfully Yours* 368) explain that Francis drew his strength for thanking God for Sister Death from the Holy Spirit, identified in the third part of the Canticle by "God's Love, Peace, Will." "This same Spirit fundamentally 'sighs' (Rom. 8:22-26). For not only does nature sigh in travail and not only do people waiting for the redemption of their bodies sigh, 'But also the Spirit of God intercedes for us with sighs too deep for words.' Francis' richly resonant final song was also preceded by this deep sighing. It is the song of one whose own body has lived through the heaviness of earth." Besides sighing, Francis was known to weep profusely.

[70]Leclerc 207.

of the new relationship Francis has experienced with this transcendent God. It is "by celebrating creatures and entering into fraternal communion with them that he rises up to the Most High and relates himself to the One whom no human words can express. What a paradox!" [71]

Francis' communion with nature is the expression of a profound detachment from self, rooted in his following the poor, humble Christ. Francis experiences the burning sun, the icy wind, the water, the bare ground by submitting to them. In this obedience to creation Francis experiences a stripping of his own self-will and a submission to his brothers and sisters of creation. *The Canticle*, uniting as it does the thrust toward the Most High and a fraternal communion with all creatures, represents a unitive grasp of reality. The most striking thing about all this is that this pacification of the human in relation with other humans "is inseparable from a very humble fraternal communion with material things themselves; the latter is the means of the former. [. . .] To be brother to all creatures, as Francis was, is in the last analysis to choose a vision of the world in which reconciliation is more important than division."[72]

This is the message of Francis' *Canticle of the Creatures*. It is rooted in the vision of universal fraternity which took him to the Sultan in peace and openness. Among the Saracens the vision was expanded and deepened. It was confirmed by the Most High on LaVerna and in the praise which burst forth in this exquisite song, now a vision of cosmic fraternity.[73]

---

[71]Leclerc 208.

[72]Leclerc 223.

[73]Leclerc (x) notes that the language Francis uses is the "ancient language typical of the sacred, language of cosmic hierophanies" (in terms strangely reminiscent of ancient pagan hymns of gratitude for the earth's maternal care). . . . This imagery transcends all religious traditions and boundaries. In his hymn, Christo-centric as it is (see Goorbergh & Zweerman), the name of Christ is never mentioned. God is referred to as "Most High" and "Lord." Surely the Muslims would have no objection to this prayer! (See appendix 2.)

Chapter V

Francis' Contribution to Interreligious Encounters and Peacemaking Today

The Wisdom of Francis

This final chapter addresses what Francis has to say to today's all important agenda of interreligious dialogue. Committed to the vision of universal fraternity, which was all the more confirmed by his experience among the Saracens, Francis spent his the rest of his life in the service of the peace which Christ came to offer the world. Francis left this world secure in the peace he described in his most sublime composition, the *Canticle of the Creatures*. His converted life was spent in helping bring about the Reign of God. The starting point in his mission was the greeting: "May the Lord give you peace." Francis knew that only with the peace of God in their hearts could people hear God's message – and thus live God's word. The world today is in desperate need of this message. Pope John Paul II presents our context in his recent Easter address.

> How many members of the human family are still subject to misery and violence! In how many corners of the world do we hear the cry of those who implore help, because they are suffering and dying: from Afghanistan,

terribly afflicted in recent months and now stricken by
a disastrous earthquake, to so many other countries of
the world where social imbalances and rival ambitions
still torment countless numbers of our brothers and sisters. [. . .] I ask you to [. . .] work so that his peace may
bring an end to the tragic sequence of atrocities and
killings that bloody the Holy Land, plunged again in
these very days into horror and despair.[1]

Four times John Paul has invited religious leaders to assemble
in Assisi, and in the "Spirit of Assisi"[2] to lead the way into peace.
Most recently he has presented this same call, at a time when it
is even more urgent.

Many religions proclaim that peace is a gift from God.
We saw this again at the recent meeting at Assisi. May
all the world's believers join their efforts to build a more
just and fraternal humanity; may they work tirelessly
to ensure that religious convictions may never be the
cause of division and hatred, but only and always a
source of brotherhood, harmony, love.[3]

Truly the spirit of Francis is alive in these words. For centuries Francis has been looked to by people and leaders of diverse
faith traditions, Christian and non-Christian, as a model for
peacemaking. This is rooted in his respect for and openness to
the other, as well as his willingness to be changed by the other.
In that stance, Francis was able to proclaim the truth of his
tradition while respecting the truth of the other, in such a way

[1]Easter Address of Pope John Paul II, March 31, 2002.

[2]Oct. 27, 1986: a summit of religious leaders to pray for peace (this
has been commemorated annually); Jan. 9-10, 1993: at the height of
the Bosnian war he summoned Christian, Muslim and Jewish leaders
to offer prayers for an end to the conflict; Oct. 25-28, 1999: a gathering
of lower level religious leaders for an Interreligious Assembly in Rome
followed by a trip to Assisi for prayer; Jan. 24, 2002: 150 representatives
from a dozen world religions gathered in Assisi to affirm that religion
can be a catalyst of reconciliation rather than of conflict and to pray for
peace. John Allen, "Together for Prayer Despite Debate," *National
Catholic Reporter* 1 February 2002: 9-11. Also see *NCR*, December 7,
2001, p. 6.

[3]Easter Address of Pope John Paul II, March 31, 2002.

as to come to an even deeper truth. Francis found that differences could be positive and even revelatory rather than harmful and isolating. Francis discovered that a new and deeper unity could be discovered within differences. Through this openness to the other Francis discovered new beauty in his own beliefs while seeing them deepened, strengthened and expanded. He was confirmed in his own tradition and found new ways to proclaim his message. The paradox was that his message seems to have been better heard by the Saracens than by his own co-religionists.

> St. Francis of Assisi walked through the Crusader battle lines near Damietta in Egypt in 1219, entering into the presence of the Kurdish ruler of Egypt, al-Malik al-Kamil, and attempted to preach to him, without any notable results. But the sultan, a son of the famous (Saladin), was impressed by the piety and simplicity of the poor man of Assisi and let him return in peace to his fellow Christians. The later career of Malik al-Kamil featured a surprising détente with the Frankish invaders of the Muslim Middle East. He even returned Jerusalem to Crusader control. It is said that he gave to the Franciscans the custody of the Christian holy places.[4]

Work in the area of interreligious dialogue has certainly underlined the truth of Francis' witness. There are various opinions as to whether the mission of Francis was successful or not. Might the exchange between Francis and the Sultan have influenced the Sultan in his on-going efforts toward peace as this author (and others) suggest?

[4]Patrick J. Ryan, "The Roots of Muslim Anger," *America*, Nov. 26, 2001 8-15. Custody of the Holy Places was actually entrusted to the Franciscan Order only in the early 14th century.

Universal Fraternity, Global Community and Ecumenical/Interreligious Dialogue[5]

The humble, submissive friar minor from Assisi stands as a powerful model for interreligious dialogue. His message of how to "go among" or "be with" the other is desperately needed today. The future of our planet depends on it. Francis offers a new possibility for today's dilemma. The "either/or" exclusive mentality which seeks "power over" must give way to a reality which embraces "the many" in a universal (fraternal) inclusivity. Gone are the days when the Christian world lived in a particular area of the globe with Muslim, Jews, Buddhists and Hindus each in their own areas. Dr. Ewert Cousins speaks of the convergence occurring today which is moving our planet into a global community:

> According to Teilhard this new global consciousness will not level all differences among peoples; rather it will generate what he calls creative unions in which diversity is not erased but intensified. [. . .] By touching each other at the creative core of their being, they release new energy, which leads to more complex units. [. . .] Throughout the process, the individual elements do not loose their identity, but rather deepen and fulfill it through union.[6]

So it is that at this time in history, the religions of the world are called to meet each other in this creative core of unions, discovering what is most authentic in each other and releasing the powerful energy each possesses for the good of the world community. William Johnston states the issue for us.

> It has become a truism to say that there can only be world peace when there is peace among the religions.

---

[5]For the purpose of this paper, I will use both terms: ecumenical (specifically Christian) and interreligious (all traditions other than Christian.) My intent is to promote unity among people of varying religious traditions by learning from the experience, example and wisdom of Francis.

[6]Ewert Cousins, *Christ of the 21st Century* (Rockport, MA: Element, 1992) 8.

Today, as never before, believers of all religions are called to love one another, to talk and listen to one another, to collaborate with one another and in this way to preserve the environment, eliminate grinding poverty, fight injustice, build a new world and lead humanity to salvation. Buddhist and Jew, Muslim and Christian, Hindu and Taoist, all must ask, "Can we work together or must we perish in a gigantic conflagration? Can we bring salvation to the world or do we die in despair?"[7]

It is obvious that the world religions have much to offer each other. Fear of the other must be replaced by the same expectant openness with which Francis approached the Sultan – in a spirit of "brother/sisterhood." Who knows what the results of that type of exchange will be? Cousins, speaking from the Christian perspective, addresses this also:

Christian theologians must be willing to reach out and enter into the very subjectivity of the other [religious] traditions in their distinct variety. [. . .] To this day Christian theology remains uninfluenced and unenriched by the majority of world religions. This is no longer possible. Our enormous store of information drawn from the history of religions, our global communication network, and the recent influence of Eastern spiritual teachers in the West are effectively breaking the envelope of isolation that has for centuries encased Christian systematic theology. When Christian consciousness opens to global consciousness, a new type of systematic theology can be born.[8]

This openness and interaction by no means intends to reduce religions to a lowest common denominator. Rather, the differences that exist are real and must be acknowledged. There is a need to be unafraid of the other's truth and to be able to affirm it as a gift for the whole. In this way, a greater self-awareness results for each tradition engaged in the dialogue and a poten-

---

[7]William Johnston, *Arise, My Love: Mysticism for a New Era* (Maryknoll: Orbis, 2000) 224.
[8]Cousins 78-79.

tial sensitivity to, appreciation for and affinity with the other religions.

Jacques Dupuis offers an interesting insight regarding the various religious traditions.

> God's saving action, which is ever at work in a unified plan, is never separated from the Christ event. [. . .] But the action of the Word is not constrained by having become historically human in Jesus Christ; nor is the work of the Spirit in history limited by being poured out by the risen Christ. The mediation of God's saving grace to humanity takes on many different aspects, which must be combined and integrated.[. . .] In fact, the different religious traditions represent "the many and various ways" God spoke and lavished himself on human beings throughout history. These religions do not so much show innumerable human efforts to seek God as they show God's continual and multiple approaches to humanity.[9]

In light of this, I would like to highlight a reference Ewert Cousins makes to Raimundo Panikkar's thoughts on Francis' *Canticle of the Creatures*.

> The Spirit of Francis' *Hymn of Brother Sun* permeates his [Raimundo's] thought. He has extended Francis' cosmic sense into the religious experience of humankind. He sings a Franciscan hymn to the fullness of creation, but he has transposed it to another key. His hymn of praise is not through Brother Sun and Sister Moon, but through Hinduism, Buddhism, Christianity, and the other great religions of the world. He rejoices in the varieties of religious experience with the same gusto with which Francis rejoiced in the varieties of flowers, animals and birds. And this joy extends to the varieties of cultures and languages, and into natural sciences and the forms of secular culture.[10]

[9]Jacques Dupuis "One God, One Christ, Convergent Ways," *Theology Digest* 47 (2000) 211-218.

[10]Cousins 74. Cousins identifies Panikkar as a cross-cultural model who is the son of a Hindu father and a Spanish, Roman Catholic mother. "He has attempted to assimilate the fullness of these traditions into

The Catholic Church and Dialogue

Since the Second Vatican Council, work toward greater unity among churches and religions has been a high priority of the Roman Church. This section will highlight some of the Church documents and principles, related to Francis' vision, which speak to this urgent project. The ecumenical and interreligious agenda of the Church is connected to the vision of Francis and the ongoing work of Franciscanism. We will first consider three interreligious/ecumenical principles of the Roman Church which are supported by Francis' vision and actions.[11] After that we will address some of the challenges this presents and the new territory to which it leads.

1. Conversion

Just as conversion was a basic element in the vocation of Francis, so too, the Roman Catholic Church identifies today's agenda for dialogue rooted in the call to conversion. Pope John Paul II has stated: "... it is urgently necessary to become aware of this most serious responsibility: today we can co-operate in proclaiming the Kingdom or we can become upholders of new divisions. May the Lord open our hearts, convert our minds and inspire in us concrete, courageous steps."[12] Foundational ecumenical documents of the Church include *Unitatis redintegratio* (*The Decree on Ecumenism*), *Nostra aetate* (*The Declaration on the Relation of the Church to Non-Christian Religions*)[13] and *Ut*

---

his personality." As a multi-dimensional man, he is a natural scientist, spiritual teacher, philosopher, theologian, and a man of prayer, sensitive to mystical intuition.

[11]Hoeberichts speaks of the mission method developed by Francis "which differed from the accepted theological opinions of his day [and which] was not at all current among his followers. In fact, it was not until after the Second Vatican Council that the originality and importance of Francis' approach to the Saracens was rediscovered" (140).

[12]John Paul II, *Orientale lumen* (Vatican City: Libreria Editrice Vaticana, 1995) 19.

[13]Hoeberichts 143: "*Nostra aetate*, promulgated on October 28, 1965, [is] the first document in the history of the Roman Catholic church which explicitly deals with the relations of the church to non-Christian religions."

unum sint (*That All May Be One*). Each document exhorts the Church to continual conversion and repentance, of which she is always in need. We recall that after Francis' experience among the lepers, he was led to do penance. Embracing a life of penance, he and his brothers are sent out to announce peace and repentance unto the forgiveness of sins. Conversion opens one to the gift of peace. *Unitatis redintegratio* states it this way:

> There can be no ecumenism worthy of the name without a change of heart. [. . .] We should therefore pray to the Holy Spirit for the grace to be genuinely self-denying, humble, gentle in the service of others, and to have an attitude of brotherly generosity towards them. . . So we humbly beg pardon of God and of our separated brethren, just as we forgive them that trespass against us (*UR* 7).

Similarly in *Nostra aetate*, we find "The Church reproves, as foreign to the mind of Christ, any discrimination . . . or harassment . . . because of race, color, . . . or religion" (*NA* 5). Regarding quarrels and hostilities between Christians and Muslims the document exhorts us to "forget the past and work sincerely for mutual understanding" in order to promote together "social justice and moral welfare, peace and freedom" (*NA* 3). *Ut unum sint* urges the same:

> Each one therefore ought to be more radically converted to the Gospel and change his or her way of looking at things . . . there is an increased sense of the need for repentance: an awareness of certain exclusions which seriously harm fraternal charity, of certain refusals to forgive, of a certain pride, of an evangelical insistence on condemning the "other side" (*UUS* 15).

Pope John Paul II, in his Apostolic Letter *Tertio millenio adveniente*, states that "among the sins which require a greater commitment to repentance and conversion [are] those which have been detrimental to the unity willed by God for his People" (*TMA* 34). This openness to conversion brings a corresponding openness to be changed by the encounter. We do not know what new awareness, truth, insight might be offered as we open ourselves to the other. Francis' life was a life of conversion, of constantly meeting God in new places/persons and of responding to God in new ways. Conversion demands a willingness to change attitudes, behaviors, and even long-held beliefs.

2. Respectful Dialogue

We saw in Francis before the Sultan a demeanor of open, honest, respectful dialogue. This is rooted in fraternal charity, profound humility and love for the truth. It requires that the two parties acknowledge each other as equals with a deep desire to listen to the other's truth, express one's own truth, and engage in conversation that will lead to new understandings and deeper truth. Burning with zeal for the Gospel, Francis longed to share this treasure with Malek al-Kamil. He approaches non-defensively. He approaches a fellow son of God, who is worthy of all the love God has given; he approaches, in short, as brother. Francis finds in this encounter that presence is equivalent to evangelization. He articulates that principle in his *Rule* upon his return to Italy (*ER*, 16.) In *Nostra aetate* we read: "The Catholic Church rejects nothing that is true and holy in these [world] religions. And She promotes dialogue and collaboration with them in order to promote good for all" (*NA* 2). "The Church regards with esteem the Muslims who adore God" (*NA* 3). "We cannot [invoke] God, Father of all, if we refuse to [conduct ourselves fraternally toward] any [person] created . . . in the image of God" (*NA* 5). How much this resonates with the words of Cardinal Walter Kasper who said: "The Christian faith, precisely in its claim of universality . . . is an appeal for and the basis of mutual tolerance and respect, of sharing and communication, of exchange and interchange, of understanding, reconciliation and peace."[14]

3. Communion/Unity

As we saw, Francis' vision of universal fraternity is ultimately a vision in which everyone and everything is intrinsically re-

[14]Walter Kasper, "Relating Christ's Universality to Interreligious Dialogue," *Centro Pro Unione Bulletin* 106 (2001/1) 88.

lated to each other.[15] This is rooted in the primacy of Christ and our relatedness to Christ: making each of us son/daughter of God and brother/sister to each other. Francis' *Canticle* gives profound expression to this. The call to restore this unity is also emphatically sounded in our documents. *Unitatis redintegratio* is clear.

> The restoration of unity among all Christians is one of the principle concerns of the Second Vatican Council. [. . . Our] division openly contradicts the will of Christ, scandalizes the world, and damages the holy cause of preaching the Gospel to every creature (1).
> Far from being an obstacle to the Church's unity, a certain diversity of customs and observances only adds to her splendor, and is of great help in carrying out her mission (16). [This applies even to differences in doctrine where in certain cases] various theological expressions are often mutually complementary rather than conflicting (17).

Nostra aetate offers similar thoughts regarding non-Christian traditions.

> In our time, when day by day mankind is being drawn closer together, and the ties between different peoples are becoming stronger, the Church examines more closely her relationship to non-Christian religions. In her task of promoting unity and love among [all people], indeed among nations, she considers above all in this declaration what [all] have in common and what draws them to fellowship. One is the community of all peoples, one their origin. . . one also is their final goal, God (1).

---

[15]John Allen [*National Catholic Reporter* (1 Feb. 2002) 10] quotes Pope John Paul II in his address to the Curia (Dec. 22, 1986): "Human beings may often not be conscious of their radical unity, and when they profess different religions incompatible among themselves, they can feel as if their divisions are insuperable. But all people are included in the grand and one design of God in Jesus Christ, who is united in a certain way with every human being, even if they are not aware of it. Every authentic prayer is called forth by the Holy Spirit, who is mysteriously present in the heart of every person." This is an allusion, obviously, to Rahner's "anonymous Christian."

Finally on this topic of unity, *Ut Unum Sint* has this to say:

> "What unites us is so much greater than what divides us" (John XXIII, 20).
> It is absolutely clear that ecumenism, the movement promoting Christian unity, is not just some sort of "appendix" which is added to the Church's teaching activity. Rather, ecumenism is an organic part of her life and work, and consequently must pervade all that she is and does (20).

Working for unity in the Catholic Church is no more an optional activity than universal fraternity was optional for Francis. The Gospel is real for Francis: we ARE one. It is a matter of reception – we have to receive this truth and embrace this way. Andrea Boni says "St. Francis' love of God became his loving reception of God's fatherhood, the Son's brotherhood and of the Spirit's communion."[16] As Francis met his brother/sister in the other, so he met God. As he met God in the other, so he saw a brother/sister. It is only fitting that Francis' *Canticle* celebrates that unity, the entire universe enveloped in communion.

The truth that Francis knew was a totally inclusive vision of reality where everything not only had a place and was related to the other, but also contributed to the whole; without which the whole was incomplete. Diversity offers the possibility for greater fullness which adds to our splendor and assists us in carrying out our mission, making possible surprising discoveries.

The harmony between humankind and creation, between male and female, reflected the inner harmony known to Francis and must be at the basis of all efforts for unity. To believe in this view of life, to live the wisdom of the *Canticle of the Creatures* is to be an ecumenical person willing to patiently, respectfully and humbly work for unity while awaiting its fullness.

Pope John Paul II has proclaimed this throughout his pontificate. Although the following is set in an ecumenical context, it expands to include interreligious dialogue as well.

---

[16]Andrea Boni, "Fraternity, Brother, Sister, Companion, New Creation," *Greyfriars Review* 10.2 (1996) 137.

Rediscovered brotherhood among Christians is one of the most precious fruits of the ecumenical dialogue. As the psalmist sings, it enables us to experience the joy of [bothers/sisters] who dwell in unity (Ps. 133:1) and makes us even more aware of how serious is the sin of division, a scandal for us and for the world. Therefore we cannot delay our steps toward the unity of the Churches. Every delay…not only risks lessening our fraternal joy, but makes us accomplices of the divisions that are growing more acute in various parts of the world. The more brotherhood is strengthened between the Churches, the more people will be encouraged in recognizing one another as brothers and sisters. Brotherhood, in fact, is an energy that knows no bounds and bears fruit for the whole human race."[17]

John Paul II has certainly furthered the work of the Second Vatican Council by taking interreligious dialogue to a new depth. He asks *how* the Holy Spirit is at work in other traditions. "Even now . . . it is fitting to pause and consider in what sense and in what ways the Holy Spirit is present in humanity's religious quest and in the various experiences and traditions that express it."[18] Johnston tells us:

Quite simply, John Paul formulates a doctrine that is patristic and traditional, even if it was forgotten for centuries: the seeds of the Word (*semina verbi*) and the groaning of the Spirit are at work in all authentic religions. In respecting other religions and their founders Christians are recognizing the action of the same Spirit who is at work in Christianity and the same Word who became flesh in Jesus of Nazareth.[19]

The Roman Church has been seriously committed to ecumenical and interreligious dialogue since the Second Vatican Council. Truly, the life and vision of Francis, 800 years prior to that

---

[17]Pope John Paul II, "Letter to Cardinal Cassidy," 11 November 1999, *Crossing the Threshold* – (2000) 68.

[18]*L'Osservatore Romano*, Sept. 16, 1998 as quoted in Johnston 225.

[19]Johnston 235.

Council, set forth the same agenda and the same approach. Does it ask even more?

Challenges and New Ground

These three principles of interreligious dialogue – conversion, respectful dialogue, and community – are truly consistent with Francis' vision and actions. However, it is imperative today that we make greater progress in understanding and appreciating differing approaches to life and to God. What more might the wisdom of Francis offer to this crucial agenda? Respect for the other was paramount for Francis. Could not a new ethic of respect take dialogue to a new place? To believe that the other (at times called "the enemy," "the infidel," or "evil") is one in whom God resides? Even if we can't "see" or "hear" the God we know? Even if we see or hear a contrary truth? Can we be respectful enough to listen to the other and to hear their truth, not necessarily embracing it as ours, but believing God could be speaking through it/them?

Is it possible to believe that we can enlarge our understanding of God through listening to the other? That we can truly find the unity we seek through letting go, surrendering, submitting to the other, in the manner of Christ and Francis, allowing ourselves to be surprised by what is given? Might we so respect the Spirit of God that we don't attempt to define how that Spirit speaks truth, brings forth justice, and acts on behalf of greater life? Could we believe that God (the same God who creates such splendid variety in creation) perhaps desires a chorus of diverse praises, arising from traditions of various religions, all united in the mystery of Christ, known or unknown? Might we teach and proclaim, first, by example, and only announce the Word "if we see that it pleases God"? Can we look at the religion of others and celebrate the presence of God in it, as Francis did? Dare we marvel and know God better?

This is the sensitivity needed for interreligious dialogue to flourish and not get stuck. This dialogue exhorts us to embrace the other as brother/sister and beloved of God and to see in them, as well as in their truths and traditions, the very presence of God. Thus it will be possible to –

. . . learn to discern the true value of the pluriformity of religions and to look at it as an invitation to journey together with other believers on their common pilgrimage to the ever-greater mystery: the most high and supreme God to whom they return all good things, wherever they find them, because they come from God who alone is good (cf. *RNB* 17:17-18; 23:9).[20]

In working toward this mutual respect and collaborative engagement, it is extremely important to respect the differences that will continue to exist. Pope John Paul said these differences must not lead to polemics or even war, as in the past. Rather, they must be accepted with humility, acknowledging the mystery of this reality which will eventually be fully revealed.

[T]here is a mystery here on which, I am certain, God will one day enlighten us. . . .I believe that, today, God invites us to change our old practices. We must respect each other and also we must stimulate each other in good works on the path of God. . . .I wish that you may be able to help in thus building a world where God may have first place, and where we, believers, give expression in our lives and in our cities to 'the most beautiful names which our religious traditions attribute to God.'[21]

The Secretariat reaffirmed those sentiments by speaking about the "age of the patience of God" in which we now live and which obliges us to wait upon God's action. "All, both Christians and the followers of other religious traditions, are invited by God . . . to enter into the mystery of his patience, as human beings seek his light and truth. Only God knows the times and stages of the fulfillment of this long human quest."[22] Hoeberichts asks if this implies that, for the time being, "we can suspend the ques-

---

[20]Hoeberichts 196.

[21]Hoeberichts 154, quoting from "The Speech of the Holy Father John Paul II to Young Muslims during his Meeting with them at Casablanca (Morocco) August 19, 1985," *Seminarium* 26 (1986) 13-22.

[22]Hoeberichts 155, quoting from *Dialogue and Proclamation*, jointly published by the Pontifical Council for Interreligious Dialogue and the Congregation for the Evangelization of Peoples, May 19, 1991.

tion of truth and salvation and entrust it to God, who wants the salvation of all humankind?"[23]

Francis is a shining model for letting God be the God of this situation. Francis, who entered into true dialogue, was filled with respect for his Muslim brothers to whom he listened attentively and spoke honestly. Francis then walked away, in faithful submission to the will of God. In that response Francis gained new insights. It appears the same gift was given to the Sultan.

Like Francis, the Church finds its faith rooted in the "spirituality of *kenosis* – of powerlessness, of continual purification from self-centeredness, of growing more in openness to our partners in dialogue."[24] It is thus that the Church is called to be a community of dialogue. Hoeberichts, relying on the work of the Asian Bishops, speaks of this new way of being church:

> Such a church is never centered on itself but on the coming true of God's dream for the world. It seeks not to exclude others but to be truly catholic in its concerns, in its appreciation of the gifts of others, and in its readiness to work with others for a world at once more human and more divine. A church that thus stands with sisters and brothers of other faiths in confronting issues of life and death will necessarily be transformed in the process.[. . .] In this model of church, dialogue, liberation, inculturation and proclamation are but different aspects of the one reality: a church that is called to be effectively a sign of reconciliation, a sign of the reign of God, a sign of the love of God...[25]

---

[23]In a February 2002 *National Catholic Reporter* article the issue of religious pluralism was identified as "perhaps the most vexing intellectual issue in the church." The article continues "The questions are not easy to formulate, notoriously difficult to answer: Is religious pluralism simply a fact of life, the way the fallen and divided world shook out? Or is it what God wants? Are other religions paths to salvation in their own right? Is the Spirit of Christ operative outside the visible bounds of Christianity? In other words, are other religions also works of the Spirit?" John Allen, "Together for Prayer Despite Debate," *National Catholic Reporter* (1 February 2002): 9-11.

[24]Hoeberichts 181.

[25]Hoeberichts 181

Which brings us back to Francis of Assisi, that living sign of reconciliation. Francis lived a message of inclusivity and communion which embraced all of creation. His most radical expression of this was his stance toward Islam and the Saracens whom he recognized and loved as brothers and sisters. Confronting the theology of a Christendom forgetful of its own tradition, he dared to proclaim a truth that had been buried – the truth of fraternal love and communion. This insight turned his life around. This is what attracted people from all strata of society: the very message of the Gospel, the mission of Christ enfleshed once again. Leonardo Boff seems to sum up the truth that Francis of Assisi lived by. It is also the guiding principle for interreligious dialogue and for bringing peace to our world. It is ultimately, of course, the message of Jesus.

> In judging our salvation or definitive damnation, God will not be guided by cultic criteria – when and how we pray – nor by doctrinal criteria – what truths we believe in. God will be guided by ethical criteria: what we did for others. The eternal destiny of human beings will be measured by how much or how little solidarity we have displayed with the hungry, the thirsty, the naked, and the oppressed. In the end we will be judged in terms of love.[26]

In the spirit of the one who fearlessly entered the camp of the "enemy" as a friend and brother, may Francis teach us today how to "be with" those who are different from us and those from whom we are alienated. For this to happen we too must choose actions on behalf of solidarity so that all might rediscover that mutual respect which leads to understanding, acceptance and peace. Francis' eloquent witness, which has long been unheard, can lead us into new ways of presence and exchange. The Paschal Mystery of Christ, Francis' only desire, *can* speak to hearts today as it spoke to and captivated Francis. Indeed, his vision of

---

[26]Leonardo Boff, *Way of the Cross, Way of Justice* (Maryknoll, NY: Orbis, 1986) 38.

universal fraternity *can* catch fire and compel us to *dare to cross new thresholds* toward global unity and peace.

Glossary

Caliph   Literally "successor" or "viceregent."

Dhikr   A prayer of remembrance of God.

Hadith   A tradition or saying traced to Muhammad; the col-
             lections of hadith comprise the literary code of the
             Prophet's Sunna, or customary practice. These are
             considered to be divinely revealed. Whereas the
             Qur'an is the direct, literal word of God, the *hadith*
             is divine revelation within Muhammad's unique
             expression.

Imam   A religious leader, in its broadest sense, a leader of
             prayer.

Islam   Complete submission/surrender to the will of God,
             which therefore brings peace.

Jihad   To strive or struggle for interior perfection; personal
             and communal discipline which lies at the core of
             Islamic spirituality.

Qur'an   The Holy Book, Sacred Scriptures of Islam. Liter-
             ally: Recite! That is, "make qur'an." Muhammad was
             commanded to write down the words of Allah
             through the Archangel Gabriel. There are 114 *suras*
             or chapters in the Qur'an.

Shahada   The Islamic profession of faith: "There is no God but
             Allah and Muhammad is the Prophet (or Messen-
             ger) of God." (This is the First Pillar of Islam.)

Salat	The ritual prayer of Muslims performed five times each day. The prayer times are called out from the minarets (towers) by a muezzin, "one who calls the prayer times." It includes a purification ritual, orientation toward Mecca (the Holy City), gestures including bowing and prostration, and the prayer. (The *salat* is the Second Pillar of Islam.)
Shi'i	A designation of the minority of Muslims (always the minority, about 10 percent today) who trace their spiritual heritage to the Prophet through his son-in-law Ali, whom they believe had been explicitly designated by Muhammad to succeed him.
Sufi	A Muslim ascetic who lived a communal life; dedicated to a stricter observance of discipline which proclaimed "There is no God but Allah and Muhammad is God's Messenger."
Sultan	Honorific title: leader.
Sunna	The example of the Prophet as reported in Muhammad's deeds, sayings and unspoken approval. The Sunna is a source of authority in Islam second only to the Qur'an. This includes the *hadith*.
Sunni	A designation of the majority of Muslims (always the majority, about 90 percent today) who backed Abu Bakr, Muhammad's father-in-law, as the legitimate leader of the Muslims. This group denied that Muhammad had designated Ali as his heir and opted for the procedure of choosing a successor from a group of elder companions of Muhammad.
Suras	Chapters in the Qur'an. There are 114 chapters contained in the Qur'an.

Appendix 1
The 99 Beautiful Names of God and The Praises of God

Names of God (99)	Arabic Word	Meaning	Praises of God
1. God *(The greatest of the 99 Names)*	Allah	The true existent, the one who unites the attributes of divinity	You are holy Lord, The only God, Who does wonders[1] (1)
2. The Infinitely Good	Al-Rahman	God's mercy is both perfect & inclusive, embracing both the deserving & undeserving; a mercy beyond the powers of people	You are the good, all good, the highest good (8)
3. The Merciful	Al-Rahim		Merciful Savior (33)
4. The King	Al-Malik	The one who has no needs, while every existing thing needs Him	You are the Almighty King (5)

[1]"Tu es sanctus Dominus Deus solus, qui facis mirabilia." *Opuscula Sancti Patris Francisi Assisiensis*, ed. Caietanus Esser, Bibliotheca Franciscana Ascetica Medii Aevi Tom. XII (Grottaferrata: Collegii S. Bonaventurae Ad Claras Aquas, 1978) 90.

5. The Holy	Al-Quddus	The one who transcends every attribute of perfection	The holy Lord God who does wonderful things (1)
6. The Flawless	Al-Salam	The one whose essence is free from defect	
7. The Faithful	Al-Mu'min	The one alone who possesses security & safety	You are security (15) You are rest (16)
8. The Guardian	Al-Muhaymin	The one who tends to every need of His creatures	You are our custodian (25)
9. The Eminent	A-'Aziz	One who is: so significant that few exist like him, for whom there is intense need as well as one to whom access is difficult	The Lord God of gods (7)
10. The Compeller	Al-Jabbar	He compels each thing & nothing compels Him	
11. The Proud	Al-Mutakabbir	The one who regards every-thing as unworthy in rela-tion to Himself	

12. The Creator	Al-Kahaliq	He is the planner of all	
13. The Producer	Al-Bari'	He initiates existence	Holy Father (6)
14. The Fashioner	Al-Musawwir	He arranges the forms of things invented in the finest way	
15. He who is full of forgiveness	Al-Ghaffar	He conceals sins and refuses to punish because of them	Merciful Savior (33)
16. The Dominator	Al-Qahhar	The one who subdues all	
17. The Bestower	Al-Wahhab	The one who gives every one what they need, expecting no recompense	You are all our riches to sufficiency (21)
18. The Provider	Al-Razzaq	The one who sustains all, outwardly & inwardly	You are all our riches to sufficiency (21)
19. The Opener	Al-Fattah	The one who opens the closed & discloses the unclear (lifts the veil)	

20. The Omniscient	Al-Alim	The one who embodies perfect knowledge & from whom knowledge is derived
21. He who contracts	Al-Qabid	The one who appropriates souls from dead bodies at death, & —
22. He who expands	Al-Basit	Extends souls to bodies at quickening
23. The Abaser	Al-Khafid	The one who banishes the evil ones, & —
24. The Exalter	Al-Rafi	Raises up the faithful
25. The Honourer	Al-Mu'izz	The one who gives dominion to whom He wills, & —
26. He who humbles	Al-Mudhill	Removes it from whom He wills
27. The All-Hearing	Al-Sami	He hears secrets & whispers & even what is more hidden than these

28. The All-Seeing	Al-Basir	The one who witnesses & sees such that nothing is remote to Him	
29. The Arbitrator	Al-Hakam	The arbitrating & avenging judge whose ruling no one overturns	You are justice (19)
30. The Just	Al-Adl	One who is the opposite of injustice & oppression	
31. The Benevolent	Al-Latif	One who combines gentleness in action & a delicacy of perception	
32. The Totally Aware	Al-Khabir	One from whom no secret is hidden	
33. The Mild	Al-Halim	One who is not roused to anger or wrath	You are moderation (20)
34. The Tremendous	Al-Azim	One who comprehends the inconceivable	Great & wonderful Lord (33)

35. The All-Forgiving	Al-Ghafur	He is the perfection & completeness of forgiveness & forgiving	Merciful Savior (33)
36. The Grateful	Al-Shakur	The One who rewards & gives eternal happiness in the next life	You are our hope (18, 28)
37. The Most High	Al-Ali	The One above whose rank there is no rank, & all are inferior to Him	You are the Most High (4) Almighty God (33)
38. The Great	Al-Kabir	The One who possesses the perfection of existence	You are Great (3) Great & wonderful Lord (33)
39. The All-Preserver	Al-Hafiz	He perpetuates the existence of all existing things & sustains them	You are our hope (18, 28)
40. The Nourisher	Al-Muqit	The One who provides nutrients for all, as in food to bodies & knowledge to hearts	You are all our riches to sufficiency (21)

41. The Reckoner	Al-Hasib	The One who suffices, for He is all one needs (and it is inconceivable that this be said of anything else)	You are all our riches to sufficiency (21)
42. The Majestic	Al-Jalil	One qualified by: might, dominion, sanctification, knowledge, wealth, power, beauty, etc.	You are beauty (13)
43. The Generous	Al-Karim	The One who unites in Himself forgiveness, fidelity, prodigal giving	You are all our riches to sufficiency (21)
44. The All-Observant	Al-Raqib	One who knows & protects with a constant gaze	You are the protector (24)
45. The Answerer of Prayers	Al-Mujib	The One who responds before being asked	
46. The Vast	Al-Wasi	The One who is expansiveness, without limit	

47. The Wise	Al-Kakim	The One who possesses wisdom; the most sublime thing of all is God	You are wisdom (10)
48. The Lovingkind	Al-Wadud	One who wishes all well & favors them (close to 'merciful')	You are love, charity (9)
49. The All-Glorious	Al-Majid	One who is noble in essence, beautiful in actions, & bountiful in gifts & favors... like 'glory'. It is as if the All-Glorious combines the Majestic, the Bestower, & the Generous	You are beauty (13) You are all our riches (21)
50. The Raiser of the Dead	Al-Ba'ith	The One who gives creatures life on the day of resurrection	You are our eternal life (32)
51. The Universal Witness	Al-Shahid	One with knowledge of visible & invisible things	

52. The Truth	Al-Haqq	One who is the antithesis of falsehood; truly existing in Himself, from which every true thing gets its true reality	
53. The Guardian (Trustee)	Al-Wakil	The One to whom everything is entrusted, fully capable of carrying them out & faithful in perfect execution	You are our guardian and defender (25)
54. The Strong	Al-Qawi	One with perfect power	You are strong (2)
55. The Firm	Al-Matin	An intensification of strength	You are strength (26)
56. The Patron	Al-Wali	One who is love and protector	You are the protector (24)
57. The Praised	Al-Hamid	One who is praised & extolled — by virtue of praise of Himself from	

eternity & His servants' praise of Him forever

No.	Name	Arabic	Description
58.	The Knower of Each Separate Thing	Al-Muhsi	The One in whose knowledge the limits of each object as well as its quantity & dimensions are revealed
59.	The Beginner, the Cause	Al-Mubdi	The One who bestows existence, (initiated creation) & —
60.	The Restorer	Al-Mu'id	Who will gather all together on the last day; for all began in Him & in Him are restored.
61.	The Life-Giver	Al-Muhyi	None is the creator of death & life but God, so He is the Life-Giver & —
62.	The Slayer	Al-Mumit	Slayer

You are security (15)

63. The Living	Al-Hayy	All existing things are under God's activity; He is the absolutely living One
64. The Self-Existing	Al-Qayyum	The One who subsists in Himself & in whom each thing subsists (Human access to this attribute is in proportion to his detachment from everything that is not God the most high.)
65. The Resourceful	Al-Wajid	The One who lacks nothing
66. The Magnificent	Al-Majid	Means the same as the All-Glorious
67. The Unique	Al-Wahid	The One who can neither be divided nor duplicated
68. The Eternal	Al-Samad	The One to whom one turns in need, who is intended in our desires; ultimate dominion culminates in Him

69. The All-Powerful	Al-Qadir	The One who possesses power
70. The All-Determiner	Al-Muqtadir	Same as above, but more emphatic
71. The Promoter	Al-Muqaddim	The One who brings close & promotes (e.g. prophets)
72. The Postponer	Al-Mu'akhkhir	The One who brings close & banishes (e.g. enemies)
73. The First	Al-Anwal	The first beginning is from Him
74. The Last	Al-Akhir	The last return & destination is to Him
75. The Manifest	Al-Zahir	He is concealed by His light & hidden by the intensity of his manifestations: He is the manifest One than whom there in none more manifest, & —

76. The Hidden	Al-Batin	the hidden One than whom none is more hidden	
77. The Ruler	Al-Wali	The One who plans the affairs of creation & governs them	
78. The Exalted	Al-Muta'ali	Means the same as the Most High (37), although it is intensified	Almighty God (32)
79. The Doer of Good	Al-Barr	The One from whom every good deed & beneficence comes	Lord God who does wonderful things (1)
80. The Ever-relenting	Al-Tawwab	The One who calls sinners to return to Him & repent, granting them favor, gain	Merciful Savior (33)
81. The Avenger	Al-Muntaqim	The One who breaks the back of the recalcitrant, punishes criminals & intensifies the punishment of the oppressor, after giving them the opportunity to change	

82. The Effacer of Sins	Al-Afu	The One who erases sins & overlooks acts of disobedience (close to the All-Forgiving, 35)	Merciful Savior (33)
83. The All-Pitying	Al-Ra'uf	The One who possesses pity, an intensification of mercy (3)	Merciful Savior (33)
84. The King of Absolute Sovereignty	Malike al-Mulk	The One who carries out what he will in His Kingdom, bringing into being & destroying, perpetuating & annihilating	Most High (4) Almighty King (5) Almighty God (33)
85. The Lord of Majesty and Generosity	Dhu'l-Jalal wa 'l-Ikram	The One from whom there is no majesty, perfection or generosity, but that it is His	You are great (3) You are the most high (4)
86. The Equitable	Al-Muqsit	The One who demands justice for the wronged from the wrongdoer	You are justice (19)

87. The Uniter	Al-Jami	The One who combines similar & dissimilar things, and opposites. (e.g. bringing many human beings together on the face of the earth)	
88. The Rich	Al-Ghani	The One who transcends connections with things other than Himself	You are all our riches to sufficiency (21)
89. The Enricher	Al-Mughni	The One who supplies what is needed	
90. The Protector	Al-Mani	The One who counters the causes of destruction & diminishment in religious & temporal affairs (39)	You are the protector (24)
91. The Punisher & —	Al-Darr	The One from whom good comes forth, benefit & harm—	

92. He who Benefits	Al-Nafi		
93. Light	Al-Nur	The visible One by whom everything is made visible (Existence is a light streaming to all things from the light of His essence.)	
94. The Guide	Al-Hadi	The One who guides the elect to a knowledge of His essence so they might call on it as a witness to things	
95. The Absolute Cause	Al-Badi	Is such that nothing similar to it is known; so He is originator eternally & forever	You, Holy Father, King of heaven and earth (6)
96. The Everlasting	Al-Baqi	Is the existent whose existence is necessary in itself	The Lord God of gods (7)

97. The Inheritor	Al-Warith	The One to whom possessions return after the possessors disappear, since He is the One who endures & to whom all returns	
98. The Right in Guidance	Al-Rashid	The One whose plans are ordered to their goals without the help of any advisor	
99. The Patient	Al-Sabur	The One who does not let haste move him to action before the right time, but rather decides matters according to plans, without being subject to a force opposing His will.	You are patient (12)

Sources:

Al-Ghazali: The Ninety-Nine Beautiful Names of God, al-Maqsad al-sana fi sharh asma'Allah al-husna, trans. David B. Burrell and Nazih Daher (Cambridge: The Islamic Texts Society, 1992).

Regis Armstrong et al., eds., *The Saint*, Vol. 1 of *Francis of Assisi, Early Documents*, (New York: New City Press, 1999) 109.

Appendix 2
Prayers

Islamic Prayers

This prayer is one of **Muhammad's** favorite:

"O God, indeed you know and see where I stand and hear what I say. You know me inside and out; nothing of me is hidden from you. And I am the lowly, needy one who seeks your aid and sanctuary, aware of my sinfulness in shame and confusion. I make my request of you as one who is poor; as a humbled sinner I make my pleas; fearful in my blindness I call out to you, head bowed before you, eyes pouring out tears to you, body grown thin for you, face in the dust at your feet. O God, as I cry out to you, do not disappoint me; but be kind and compassionate to me, you who are beyond any that can be petitioned, most generous of any that give, most merciful of those who show mercy [a reference to Qur'an 12]. Praise to God, Lord of the universe."[1]

Another prayer of **Muhammad's**, for the healing of the sick:

God, our Lord, you who are in the heavens, may your name be sanctified. Yours is the command in the heavens and on earth. As your mercy is in the heavens, so let your mercy be on earth. Forgive our sins and failures. You are the Lord of those who seek to do good. Upon

---

[1]Renard, *101 Questions on Islam* 67.

this illness send down mercy from your mercy and healing from your healing."[2]

A prayer **Muhammad** prayed for himself:

O God, guide me among those you have guided, and sustain me among those you have sustained. Make me your intimate friend among those you have made your intimate friends. Bless me in what you have given me.

Another prayer of **Muhammad**:

"O God, create light in my heart, and light in my eye, and light in my hearing, and light on my right, and light on my left, light above me, light below me, light in front of me, light behind me. Create light for me: on my tongue, light; in my muscles, light; in my flesh, light; in my hair, light; in my body, light; in my soul, light. Make light grow for me. O God, grant me light!"[3]

A prayer of **Muhammad** as he performed the prostration, which others are encouraged to use:

"Before Thee I prostrate myself, in Thee I believe, to Thee I am surrendered. My face is prostrate before Him who created it and moulded it and pierced for it (the openings of) hearing and sight. Blessed Be God the Best of Creators."[4]

The martyr-mystic **al-Hallaj** (d. 922) describes his awareness of God who is all around and within:

"O God, the sun neither rises nor sets but that your love is one with my breathing. Never have I sat in conversation, but that it was you who spoke to me from among those seated round. Never have I been mindful of you, either in sadness or rejoicing, but that you were there in my heart amidst my inmost whisperings. Never have

---

[2]Renard, *101 Questions on Islam* 69.
[3]Renard, *101 Questions on Islam* 69.
[4]Renard, *Seven Doors to Islam* 39.

I decided on a drink of water in my thirst, but that I saw your image in the cup."

"**Rumi**, [the famous Sufi mystic] tells a story about a man who prayed devoutly, keeping vigil late into the night. Once when he began to tire and weaken in his resolve to persevere, Satan saw his chance and planted a suggestion in his weary soul. For all your calling out "O God," have you ever once heard God reply "Here I am"? The man had to admit he had never detected even a faint whisper in reply. God took note of all this and sent a messenger to the praying man. All of the fear and love the man had poured into his invocation, the messenger assured him, were already God's gift, unrequested and unrealized. "Beneath every 'O Lord' of yours, lies many a 'Here I am' from me." No one seeks God but that God has first planted the desire to seek; the answer is prior to the question."[5]

Renard reminds us that in many aspects of Islamic spiritual life, **Abraham** sets the example. "Rumi notes that where there is no sighing, there is no ecstasy; and Abraham was the "sighful man" par excellence. When the patriarch prayed, his personal commitment and intensity caused his heart to bubble. You could hear Abraham praying for miles."[6]

Nazir ad-Din (13th century) explains the spiritual meaning of the ablution prior to ritual prayer. This speaks to 'right intention.'

"When the person finishes the ablution and aims to say the ritual prayer, he should turn away from all things to the extent possible. He should make his heart present and be aware of the tremendousness and majesty of God. He should understand that he will be talking intimately with the Sultan of sultans. Since he has purified the parts of himself where creatures look with outward water, he should also purify the place where God looks

---

[5]Renard, *101 Questions on Islam* 68.
[6]Renard, *101 Questions on Islam* 67.

– which is called the "heart" – with the water of turning
toward God, repenting, and asking forgiveness. If he does
not do this, he is like someone who wants to bring the
sultan into his home. He cleans the outside of the house,
but he leaves the inside of the house – the place where
the sultan will sit – full of filth. We seek refuge in God
like that! 'God looks not at your forms, not at your works,
but He looks at your hearts.'"[7]

A Prayer of **Rabia**:

O God,
Whenever I listen to the voice of anything you have made
The rustling of the trees
The trickling of water
The cries of birds
The flickering of shadow
The roar of the wind
The song of the thunder,
I hear it saying:
God is One!
Nothing can be compared with God![8]

[7]Renard, *Seven Doors to Islam* 40.

[8]Maria Jaoudi, *Christian and Islamic Spirituality: Sharing a Journey*
(Mahwah: Paulist Press, 1993) 84.

Prayers of Francis

The *Canticle of the Creatures*[1]

Most High, all-powerful, good Lord,
Yours are the praises, the glory, and the honor,
    and all blessing,
To You alone, Most High, do they belong,
And no human is worthy to mention Your name.

Praised be You, my Lord, with all Your creatures,
Especially Sir Brother Sun,
Who is the day and through whom You give us light,
And he is beautiful and radiant with great splendor;
And bears a likeness of You, Most High One.

Praised be You, my Lord, through Sister Moon
    and the stars,
In heaven You formed them clear and precious
    and beautiful.
Praised be You, my Lord, through Brother Wind,
And through the air, cloudy, and serene, and every
    kind of weather,
Through whom You give sustenance to Your creatures.
Praised be You, my Lord, through Sister Water,
Who is very useful and humble and precious and chaste.
Praised be You, my Lord, through Brother Fire,
    through whom You light the night,
And he is beautiful and playful and robust and strong.
Praised be You, my Lord,
    through our Sister Mother Earth,
Who sustains and governs us
And who produces various fruit with colored flowers
    and herbs.

Praised be You, my Lord, for those who give pardon
    for Your love,
And bear infirmity and tribulation.
Blessed are those who endure in peace
For by You, Most High, they shall be crowned.

[1]*FA:ED* 1, 113.

Praised be You, my Lord, for our Sister Bodily Death,
From whom no one living can escape.
Woe to those who die in mortal sin.
Blessed are those whom death will find
     in Your most holy will,
For the second death shall do them no harm.

Praise and bless my Lord and give Him thanks
And serve Him with great humility.

The *Praises of God*[2]

You are the holy Lord God, [the only One,]
who does wonderful things.

You are strong. You are great. You are the most high.
You are the almighty king. You Holy Father,
King of heaven and earth.

You are three and one, the Lord God of gods;
You are the good, all good, the highest good,
Lord God living and true.

You are love, charity; You are wisdom, You are humility,
You are patience, You are beauty, You are meekness,
You are security, You are rest,
You are gladness and joy, You are our hope,
You are justice,
You are moderation, You are all our riches to sufficiency.

You are beauty, You are meekness,
You are the protector, You are our custodian
and defender,
You are strength, You are refreshment. You are our hope,
You are our faith, You are our charity,
You are all our sweetness, You are our eternal life:
Great and wonderful Lord, Almighty God,
Merciful Savior.

[2]*FA:ED* 1, 109. The phrase "the only One" is translation of the author.

Bibliography

Primary Sources

Assisi Compilation. From *Francis of Assisi: Early Documents* Vol. II, ed. Regis J Armstrong, J.A. Wayne Hellmann and William J. Short. New York: New City Press, 2000.

Bonaventure of Bagnoregio. *The Major Legend of St. Francis*. From *Francis of Assisi: Early Documents* Vol. II, ed. Regis J Armstrong, J.A. Wayne Hellmann and William J. Short. New York: New City Press, 2000.

Jordan of Giano, Thomas of Eccleston, Salimbene degli Adami. *XIIIth Century Chronicles*. Trans. Placid Hermann. Chicago: Franciscan Herald Press, 1961.

Francis of Assisi. *Earlier Exhortation to the Clergy, The First Letter to the Custodians, A Letter to the Rulers of the People, The Letter to the Entire Order, The Earlier Rule, The Praises of God, A Blessing for Brother Leo, The Canticle of the Creatures*. From *Francis of Assisi: Early Documents* Vol. I, ed. Regis J Armstrong, J.A. Wayne Hellmann and William J. Short. New York: New City Press, 1999.

Thomas of Celano. *The Life of St. Francis*. From *Francis of Assisi: Early Documents*. Vol. I, ed. Regis J Armstrong, J.A. Wayne Hellmann and William J. Short. New York: New City Press, 1999.

Thomas of Celano. *The Remembrance of the Desire of a Soul.*
From *Francis of Assisi: Early Documents* Vol. II, ed. Regis
J Armstrong, J.A. Wayne Hellmann and William J. Short.
New York: New City Press, 2000.

Secondary Sources

Al Faruqi, Isma'il Rajied. *Trialogue of the Abrahamic Faiths:
Papers presented to the Islamic Studies Group of Ameri-
can Academy of Religion.* 4th ed. Beltsville, Md: Amana,
1995 (1415 AH).

Alavi, Karima Diane. "Turning to the Islamic Faith." *America* 4
March 2002: 188-20.

Baagil, H.M. *Muslim Christian Dialogue.* Riyadh, Saudi Arabia:
International Islamic Publishing House, 1984.

Basetti-Sani, Giulio. *Muhammad, St. Francis of Assisi and
Alvernia.* Manila: Franciscan Institute of Asia, 1979.

Basetti-Sani, Guilio. *For a Dialogue Between Christians and
Muslims.* Reprinted from *The Muslim World.* Hartford
Seminary Foundation LVII, No. 3, 1967.

Boff, Leonardo. *Way of the Cross – Way of Justice.* Maryknoll:
Orbis, 1986.

Bonanno, Raphael, ed. *Jews, Moslems and Christians: Children
of God.* Jerusalem: Franciscan Printing Press, 1988.

Boni, Andrea. "Fraternity, Brother, Sister, Companion, New Creation." *Greyfriars Review* 10.2 (1996): 135-151.

Borrmans, Maurice. *Guidelines for Dialogue Between Christians
and Muslims.* Trans. R. Marston Speight. Mahwah, NJ:
Paulist Press, 1981.

Bryant, M. Darrol and S. A. Ali, ed. *Muslim-Christian Dialogue:
Promise and Problems.* St. Paul: Paragon House, 1998.

Camps, Arnulf, et al. *Islam and the Friars Minor*. Trans. Rolph Fernandes and Philippe Yates. Rome: General Curia, OFM, 1991.

Cusato, Michael F. "Hermitage or Marketplace? The Search for an Authentic Franciscan Locus in the World." *True Followers of Justice: Identity, Insertion, and Itinerancy among the Early Franciscans*. Ed. Elise Saggau. Spirit and Life. Vol. 10. St. Bonaventure: Franciscan Institute, 2000.

Cusato, Michael F. "The Renunciation of Power as a Foundational Theme in Early Franciscan History." *The Propagation of Power in the Medieval West*. Ed. A.A. McDonald. Mediaevalia Groningana 23. Groningen: Egbert Forsten, 1997.

Cousins, Ewert H. *Christ of the 21ˢᵗ Century*. Rockport, MA: Element, 1992.

De Beer, Francis. "St. Francis and Islam." *Francis of Assisi Today*. Ed. Christian Duquoc and Casiano Floristan. Concilium 149. New York: Seabury, 1981.

De Beer, Francis. *We Saw Brother Francis*. Trans. Maggi Despot and Paul LaChance. Chicago: Franciscan Herald Press, 1983.

Dupuis, Jacques. "One God, One Christ, Convergent Ways." *Theology Digest* 47 (Fall 2000): 211-218.

Esposito, John L. *Islam: The Straight Path*. 3ʳᵈ ed. New York: Oxford University Press, 1998.

Esposito, John L., ed. *The Oxford History of Islam*. New York: Oxford University Press, 1999.

Fleming, John. "The Iconographic Unity of the Blessing for Brother Leo." *Franziskanische Studien* 63 (1981): 203-220.

Flood, David. "Assisi's Rules and People's Needs." *Franciscan Digest* 2.2 (1992): 69-89.

Flood, David and Thaddée Matura. *The Birth of a Movement: A Study of the First Rule of St. Francis.* Chicago: Franciscan Herald Press, 1975.

Frassetto, Michael and David R. Blanks. *Western Views of Islam in Medieval and Early Modern Europe.* New York: St. Martin's Press, 1999.

Gabrieli, Francesco. *Arab Historians of the Crusades.* Trans. E.J. Costello. New York: Dorset, 1989.

Gamberoni, Sylvia Marie. "The Canticle of Brother Sun." *The Cord* 48.6 (1998): 285-291.

Godet-Calogeras, Jean François. "When 'Pace' Meets 'Salaam'." *Tau* (India) 20.4 (1995): 118-120.

Goorbergh, Edith van den, and Zweerman, Theodore. *Respectfully Yours, Signed and Sealed, Francis of Assisi: Aspects of His Authorship and Focuses of His Spirituality.* St. Bonaventure: Franciscan Institute, 2001.

Hoeberichts, J. *Francis and Islam.* Quincy: Franciscan Press, 1997.

Hoeberichts, J. "Solidarity and Service: Dialogue in Franciscan Perspective." *Franciscan Digest* 7.1 (1997): 11-28.

Jeusset, Jean Gwénolé. *God Is Courtesy.* Trans. Carolyn Frederick (n.p., n.d.).

Jaoudi, Maria. *Christian and Islamic Spirituality: Sharing a Journey.* Mahwah: Paulist Press, 1993.

John Paul II. *Easter Address.* Vatican City, March 31, 2002. <http://www.zenit.org.>

John Paul II. "Letter to Cardinal Cassidy, 11 November 1999." *Crossing the Threshold* – 2000 103 (2000/1): 68-69.

John Paul II. *Orientale lumen.* Vatican City: Libreria Editrice Vaticana, 1995.

John Paul II. *Ut unum sint.* Boston: St. Paul Books & Media (n.d.).

Johnston, William. *"Arise, My Love. . ." Mysticism For a New Era*. Maryknoll, NY: Orbis, 2000.

Kasper, Walter. "Relating Christ's Universality to Interreligious Dialogue." *Centro Pro Unione Bulletin* 106 (2001/1): 77-88.

Kedar, Benjamin. *Crusade and Mission: European Approaches Toward the Muslims*. Princeton, Princeton University Press, 1984.

Laiou, Angeliki E. and Roy P. Mottahedeh, ed. *The Crusades From the Perspective of Byzantium and the Muslim World*. Washington: Dumbarton Oaks, 2001.

Lapsanski, Duane. "The *Chartula* of St. Francis of Assisi." *Archivum Franciscanum Historicum* 67 (1974): 18-37.

Leclerc, Eloi. The *Canticle of Creatures: Symbols of Union*. Trans. Matthew O'Connell. Chicago: Franciscan Herald Press, 1977.

Lehmann, Leonhard. "Francis's Two Letters to the Custodes: Proposals for Christian-Islamic Ecumenism in Praising God." *Greyfriars Review* 2:3 (1988): 63-91.

Lehmann, Leonhard. "The Letter of Saint Francis to the Rulers of the Peoples: Structures and Missionary Concerns." *Franciscan Digest* 4.2 (1994): 25-62.

Maalouf, Amin. *The Crusades Through Arab Eyes*. Trans. Jon Rothschild. New York: Schocken Books, 1984.

Mascarenhas, Louis. "By Divine Inspiration . . . Going Among Muslims." *Franciscan Digest* 7.1 (1997): 29-37.

Maier, Christopher T. *Preaching the Crusades: Mendicant Friars and the Cross in the Thirteenth Century*. Cambridge: Cambridge U. Press, 1994.

Martin, Richard C. *Islamic Studies: A History of Religions Approach*. Upper Saddle River, NJ: Prentice Hall, 1996.

Mastnak, Tomaz. *Crusading Peace: Christendom, The Muslim World, and Western Political Order*. Berkeley: University of California Press, 2002.

Munir, Fareed. "Islam and Franciscanism: Prophet Mohammad of Arabia and St. Francis of Assisi in the Spirituality of Mission." *Islam and Franciscanism: A Dialogue*. Ed. Daniel Dwyer and Hugh Hines. Spirit and Life. Vol. 9. St. Bonaventure: Franciscan Institute, 2000.

Nanji, Azim A., ed. *The Muslim Almanac*. NY: Gale Research Inc., 1996.

Natali, A. "Gli Arabi e S. Francesco alle Crociate." *L'Italia Francescana* 33 (1958): 154-162.

Polanco, Dennis. "Francis of Assisi: A Profound Witness of Unity." *Propositum* 5.1 (2000): 40-44.

Powell, James M. *Anatomy of a Crusade: 1213-1221*. Philadelphia: University of Pennsylvania Press, 1986.

Renard, John. *In the Footsteps of Muhammad: Understanding the Islamic Experience*. Mahwah: Paulist Press, 1992.

Renard, John. *Responses to 101 Questions on ISLAM*. Mahwah: Paulist Press, 1998.

Renard, John. *Seven Doors to Islam: Spirituality and the Religious Life of Muslims*. Berkeley: University of California Press, 1996.

Renard, John. *Windows on the House of Islam: Muslim Sources on Spirituality and Religious Life*. Berkeley: University of California Press, 1998.

Roncaglio, Martiniano. *St. Francis of Assisi and the Middle East*. 3rd ed. Cairo: Franciscan Center of Oriental Studies, 1957.

Rotzetter, Anton. "Francis of Assisi: A Bridge to Islam." *Concilium* 1999/2: 107-115. Maryknoll, Orbis.

Ryan, Patrick J. "The Roots of Muslim Anger." *America* Nov. 26, 2001. 8-15.

Schimmel, Annemarie. *Mystical Dimensions of Islam.* Chapel Hill: University of North Carolina Press, 1975.

Schmucki, Octavian. "St. Francis of Assisi, Messenger of Peace in His Time." *Greyfriars Review* 9.2 (1995): 147-162.

Tolan, John Victor, ed. *Medieval Christian Perceptions of Islam: A Book of Essays.* New York: Garland, 1996.

Vatican Council II. *Nostra aetate* (28 October 1965). Ed. Walter M. Abbott. *The Documents of Vatican II.* New York: Guild Press, 1966. 660-668.

Vatican Council II. *Unitatis redintegratio* (21 November 1964). Ed. Walter M. Abbott. *The Documents of Vatican II.* New York: Guild Press, 1966. 341-366.

Videos

Attitude of Islam toward Christianity. Ahmad Zahi Yamani. Islamic Information Service, 1998.

Islam: Empire of Faith. Gardner Films, distributed by PBS, 2000.

Islam: The Faith and the People. Brown-Roa, 1991.

Mosque. Hallel Communications, Maryknoll, 1992.